ISBN 978-0-359-23866-8

Mister, Are You a Lady?

Roi Barnard

Note from the Author

Actress Sarah Jessica Parker once said, "I have always loved to read for the same reason I love to act, which is that other people's stories are more interesting to me than my own."

On a talk show discussing her autobiography, Actress Sophia Loren stopped the show's hostess, looked out at the audience and said, "Looking at your faces, I know your lives have been more interesting than mine, I am just well known."

After 50 years of listening to my clients' and friends' stories and telling them about my past, they've convinced me that my story is interesting too. I hope you agree. I promise to read yours!

-   *Roi Barnard*

Dedicated

To all boys and girls who are in distress with their gender on sexual identity. Be honest with yourself. It is so scary but times have gotten better. If I could do it 70 years ago, I am sure with love you will be just fine.

Forward

"MISTER, ARE YOU A LADY?"

The *year* was 1972, I was wearing a cowboy hat, a tank top, very short shorts, platform shoes that made me even taller than my natural 6 feet, a belt with a large silver buckle and lots of jewelry. Just back from Jamaica, *sporting* a beautiful tan, I leaned over for a carton of milk in the Georgetown Safeway, AKA "The Social Safeway" grocery store in Washington DC. I felt a pinch on the back of my leg, looked down *and* saw a *beautiful* little boy; blonde hair, big blue eyes, about 5 years old, looking *up* at me.

"Mister, are you a lady?" he repeated.

I kneeled down to his level and explained.

"*No.* I'm a boy just like you. Ladies don't usually have big mustaches like I do."

At that point his embarrassed mother, equally as beautiful, arrived and pulled him away with an apologetic groan *saying*, "Please don't tell me, I can only imagine!"

I assured her we had come to terms.

I have often thought of this child and his mother, *thinking* what a great

title for a book! I remember thinking *also* that perhaps I should start

toning down my dress in public, but it was too late. As a gay, male model

from the south, I was *already* on the road to much greater infamy in the

PAPER city of Washington DC. So I marched on.

Chapter 1

Already a Sissy

I looked up at Mama and asked, "Why is Buddy sleeping in the bathtub with his good clothes on?" I was 5 years old and didn't realize that my brother Buddy, who was 7 and had been sickly from birth, had died of pneumonia. The year was 1941, war time and medicine short in supply.

"He has to go away for a while, Roy," Mama said, "but you'll see him again one day." She repeated that story to me until I was old enough to realize that he had gone to heaven.

Losing Buddy was the beginning of a long, hard journey for me. The struggle to acquire love from my father, Willie, began in that moment. I became a constant reminder to him of the boy who had left us far too soon. Buddy was Willie's favorite. I know now that he was afraid to love me in case I too left him. So, he switched off his love valve.

After Buddy died, I refused to go to bed alone. I wanted the doll I'd seen in Mr. Johnson's drug store window to keep me company. She was as tall as I was and beautiful, with big blue glass eyes, blond hair, and a pale blue dress with dark blue ribbons. I wanted that doll more than anything.

I didn't just want her, I needed her. Every time I went to the store, I ran to look at her. My father said to me, "If you get that doll you will grow up to be a sissy." Neither one of us knew at the time that it was too late. I was already a sissy. Que Sera Sera.

However, one night I threw such a fit that my Mama told my father Willie, " I am getting that doll for Roy, sissy or not!" She called Mr. Johnson and had him open his store so I could have the doll to sleep with in the place of my brother. When Mama came home with that doll, I was so happy. I named her Lana, for Mama's favorite movie star. I used to choose dresses from my Lana Turner coloring books and ask Mama to sew them for my doll. I was already a designer of fashion.

One day I looked out the window and saw my precious doll sitting under a tree, where my cousin, Betty, had left her. Lana had been destroyed by the rain that had fallen the night before. I told my mother that Lana had to go away like Buddy did and I wanted to bury her in the backyard with my dog, Maxwell. So Mama found a big white box. We tied a huge red ribbon around it and we buried Lana in the backyard. I cried for a while, but I knew it was time to let Lana go. I never longed for another doll but I wasn't interested in cars, trains, or sports either.

Buddy, Tillie, and Roy in 1938

Later in life I did develop a keen interest in antique cars, like Bentleys and Rolls Royce's. But more about these rides later.

My mama – her name was Tillie – and Willie struggled for a while after Buddy died. Mama was overprotective of me, and Willie, who was lost and broken, began to drink. He became abusive toward me, physically and mentally, whenever no one else was around, so I tried hard not to find myself alone with him. I was afraid of him and I did not like my dad very much at the time. He wasn't easy to like. I found myself hiding a lot and wanting to be alone. I felt safe alone.

One day, Dad was telling a story at my Uncle Vannie's house. I was 7 years old sitting on the porch railing and interrupted my dad to tell him he was getting the story all wrong. "That wasn't the way it happened," I said. I proceeded to tell my version when all of a sudden, Willie jumped up and in his anger knocked me off the railing and into my Aunt Eva's rosebush garden below. It was a hot summer day and I was just wearing a pair of shorts, no shoes or shirt. When I got up, I was scratched and bleeding from my arms, face, chest, and legs. At the time, we lived around the block from my Uncle and Aunt in Norfolk, Virginia, and I ran home as fast as I could, crying all the way.

Mama grabbed me when I walked in the door. We both cried as I told her what happened. After cleaning me up, she gathered some clothes, called my Aunt Elizabeth in Newport News, Virginia, and asked if we could come stay for a while. My aunt told us to come right away. Mama took my hand and we ran to the Trailways bus station and traveled to my aunt's house. I was very quiet!

We stayed with my aunt for quite a while. Willie would call every couple of days and tell Mama how sorry he was, to please come back, that he would behave better. But Tillie said "No, I don't trust you. You cannot do this to Roy!"

My mother would dress me up in a little white sailor suit and we would walk downtown Norfolk together. The sailors would salute me and talk to me and my mom, who was a beautiful woman. I was a pretty, little boy and really enjoyed the attention I got from those guys, even at the tender age of seven!

One day Willie showed up at my aunt's house. Mama sent me to another room. She left the house with my father but told me she would be back soon. Willie took Mama to dinner and they were gone for quite a while. When they came back Mama told me we were going home and that I was to be a good boy and try not to upset my father. Tillie really loved Willie. I was really scared but I trusted my mom so much.

For several days I was still frightened of Willie and I kept my distance. It was at this time that I became a quieter, more thoughtful, little boy. I often sought out rocking chairs or the swing we had in the backyard. I spent a lot of my time during the next few years thinking and hiding from Willie.

I didn't know it then but before we returned home, Mama made Willie promise never to touch me again. He never did, but he was psychologically abusive to me throughout most of our lives together, up until he was an old man.

A couple of years later, around the end of World War II, we moved into a small, red house in Poplar Branch, North Carolina. The village *was* near where my dad was born; population about 300. The kitchen was separated from the main part of the house by a porch, which in those days was called a summer kitchen. We had no indoor plumbing, but neither did anyone else living on our dirt road. All our outside toilets were lined up at the back of our houses in a perfect, straight line from property to property. I always found that interesting.

I always hated those outhouses. They were filled with strange bugs, stinging bees, and snakes. I used to think my grandmother was rich because her outhouse was painted and insulated. It had a window to the outside, and she'd sewn curtains for the window. She lived three miles from us so when I could I would ride my bike to use her fancy outhouse instead of ours. Prissy came early for me.

I spent a week each summer with my Aunt Eva and Uncle Vannie, in Norfolk, Virginia. I thought they were rich because they had an indoor bathroom. They had a huge white bathtub in their home. Aunt Eva had to tell me that one bath a day was enough and that I did not need to have two or three a day. I loved the fact that I could stretch out in that tub from head to toe, but promised her I would only take one bath a day. I loved feeling so clean having spent so many years of bathing in a washtub throughout my childhood only after all my younger siblings had bathed in the water first. By the time it was my turn, I would never come out feeling clean. That's just the way it was.

Later in life I was overjoyed to be able to install a bathroom at Mama's house. It took over half the back porch and included a tub, shower, commode, sink, and bright yellow linoleum. The only fly in the ointment was that the door went straight into the dining room. That was a bit odd but compared to the outhouse no one could complain. My mother cried with happiness and told me she felt like Queen Elizabeth. Willie actually helped build it, but he refused to use that indoor bathroom at first. He kept going off to the outhouse until one cold evening Tillie said, "You know Willie, you're just a damn fool. Why are you so stubborn? Roy wanted this bathroom to be for you too. It's freezing outside. Why do you still keep going out to the outhouse?" Willie took his coat off and used indoor plumbing for the first time.

He never used the outhouse again, and he eventually tore it down. In hindsight I think Willie was just angry that it was I who put the bathroom in and that he hadn't been able to do that for his family. He felt bad about it. But I didn't care. I just wanted Mama and my siblings to have indoor plumbing.

Chapter 2

Hand to Fist

"Tillie honey, can you give me a quick haircut?" I recall hearing those words from a very early age as people came to our kitchen door to ask for my mother's hair services – a trim, a perm, or color. My mother was what we called a kitchen cutter, the local hairdresser, even though she was never trained or licensed to do this work. She just knew how to do it. More importantly, she loved people. From the age of 5, Mama paid me a nickel to sweep the hair from the back porch in the summer and the kitchen in the winter. I loved what happened on that back porch, the camaraderie and conversations. That's when I first got interested in the hairdressing and beauty business.

Sometimes she would trade a cut or a perm for eggs, milk, vegetables, or chicken feed bags, which she used to make pajamas for us children. Back then perms stunk of ammonia and my dad would come home and shout "Not another perm, Tillie! It smells so bad in here!"

Mama was also the town dressmaker and she baked beautiful cakes for all occasions. She was well-loved in our community, almost like the mother of our entire town. She did all she could to bring in money for the family. Eventually there was a road named for my mom called, "Tillie Lane".

Bittersweet!

We were very poor but we were never hungry. We had food and we had love. My dad never made much money. Willie was well liked by his friends, the "good ole' boys," but he had a slight drinking problem. He wasn't mean, however, when he drank too much. On the contrary, he became very funny and made all his kids laugh (except for me, ever watchful), as Mama would try to get him dressed and ready for bed. He liked to make jokes about it, but it wasn't funny to me because I was the one Mama sent to find him when he indulged and to bring him home.

I can still hear the men at Mr. JJ Bunch's General Merchandise Store, when they would see me coming. They would say, "Old boy Bill...you're in deep trouble now. Here comes that boy of yours." I was maybe 12 years old at the time. I would appear in front of all those men with my hands on my hips and say, "Daddy, Mama said for you to come home right now. You hear?" All the guys would say, "We told you Bill. When your boy comes, you better move." So Willie would get up and I would help him get home. I don't think that helped our relationship much, but I was a mama's boy and I did what she told me to.

Tillie, the hairdresser in 1944 and Roy, her assistant with broom in hand

Many times Willie would forget to give my mother school lunch money for my brothers and sisters. I would jump from the breakfast table and run outside to catch him and say, "Excuse me, but you forgot something." Willie would say, "What you talking about boy?" And I would reply, "You forgot money for my brothers' and sisters' lunches." Willie would take his wallet and throw it on the ground saying, "Take what you need." I would take his money and then throw his wallet back on the ground. This did not help our relationship either, but I knew he would never touch me so I took liberties like that. We played these games with each other for many years.

As soon as I was able, I would do anything to make money to help Mama. When I was 7 or 8, my grandmother hired me to wash eggs from her chicken farm. I loved it. I would sit on the back porch with my grandmother and we would wash eggs together and crate them. She would pay me 10 cents a crate. A crate held 24 dozen eggs, so I made a dime for every 288 eggs I washed. The egg man would come every Thursday morning to pick up the eggs and pay my grandmother and she would then pay me. I sat there hour after hour, talking to my grandmother as she dipped snuff and listened to her stories.

As Grandma dipped her snuff – placing the tobacco between her gum and her lower lip – I would dip into a box of raw Jell-o with an ice cream spoon and the powder would bubble up in my mouth. To this day I occasionally put a spoonful of raw Jell-o powder in my mouth just to recall that sensation. And every time my grandmother spat into her cuspidor, I would spit into a coffee can. Sitting on the back porch washing eggs with my grandmother is one of my favorite childhood memories.

We were talking about names one day and my grandmother said, "I went to school with a girl named Elizabeth Melissy North Carolina Brown.'" "What did you call her, Gram?" I asked. She answered coyly, "Oh, we just called her NC!" We laughed so hard I almost broke an egg.

When I was older, I graduated from washing eggs to picking tomatoes, digging potatoes, and plucking okra on a farm. I hated plucking okra. It was very sticky, and I had to pick it in the late afternoon when the air was cooler and the okra was firmer and easier to pick. Unfortunately it was when the gnats came out as well. It was an uncomfortable job all around but it paid good money. I made 10 cents an hour to pick that okra and I considered myself lucky. I liked my boss. He was kind to me and he knew I was a hard worker. He was born and raised in Poplar Branch. I worked for lots of farmers back then. They were all very nice to me and I tried to be a very loyal, hard worker at an early age.

After working in the field all day, while there was still daylight, I mowed yards and did anything else to help contribute to the family. Mama made money making dresses and other clothes for people in our community. She had to make a payment every month to keep her sewing machine. One time she got behind and the Singer Sewing people came to repossess her sewing machine. I was 12 years old and I ran from the house crying and hid behind the barn. I stayed there, feeling so sad for my mother. She was able to get it back in couple of weeks, but that feeling of helplessness because of not having what we needed stuck with me. I vowed to make life easier for her one day. And I did.

Eventually our family grew to include my brothers Jackie, Randy and Billy and my sister Georgia. It was as if my parents were making up for their loss of Buddy. Tillie had her last child when I was 19. She was very upset when she found out she was pregnant because she thought she was too old – 44 – to have another child. But this last baby was a precious gift, the gentlest of human beings, who would become Willie's and Tillie's angel on earth during their aging years. My mom let me name him Michael Ray. I loved him so much!

Michael Ray looked like a reincarnation of my first brother, Buddy, fulfilling in a way my mom's promise that I would see him again. He was even sickly like Buddy had been and was allergic to many things when he was born, including milk. Eventually, he succumbed to disease. I lost my first brother, Buddy, to pneumonia when he was 7, and my youngest brother, Michael Ray, to cancer when he was 57. There are five of us siblings still living and we are very close.

After leaving Poplar Branch for DC at the age of 19, I often returned to North Carolina to see my family. I missed watching my brothers and sisters grow up because I was so much older than most of them and I was always aware of my desire to help them as much as possible. I became Santa Claus and surrogate father to my siblings and I could never do enough for my mother, with whom I always had a special bond.

Chapter 3

Small Town Drama

In addition to us seven siblings, my mother also raised one of her nieces because her mother had died. Madeleine was her name – we called her Madge – and we became very close and still are today. I was 9 when she arrived and she was 12. She was a big help to me during my pre-teen and teen years.

I first realized I was different when Madge's boyfriend came to the house to court her and he started wrestling with me. I became aroused. It scared me and excited me at the same time. I fell hopelessly in love with him. He was 9 or 10 years older than me and sensed my attraction so he kept me at arm's distance from that day on.

When Madge was going to her first prom, my mother made her a beautiful gown. It was pale blue satin with a blue chiffon overlay. It was strapless and showed off Madge's generous bosom! One day I went into her room and decided to try the gown on. I got it on and it fit just fine, but then I let my breath out and the gown ripped all the way down the back along the zipper. I was so upset and scared. When Madge came home, she came to my room with the dress and accused me of putting it on. I tried to lie my way out of the situation but she had my number. I begged her not to tell my mother and especially not my father. She was kind and agreed to not to tell anyone but I paid her 50 cents a week until I had paid $5. To this day my darling Madge and I get a good laugh out of that story. I love her so much!

I knew from then on that I was very much more into boys than girls. Between age 10 and 14, I had sexual experiences with boys in my town, always a couple of years older than me. I felt what we were doing was wrong but I couldn't stop my feelings. To this day I recall the things we used to do in the duck blinds, barns, over garages, anywhere we wouldn't get caught.

Once when I was 13 years old, a married guy I was working for took me to his house and into their bed with him. He said, "You know Willie would kill me." I said "Yes, but he would kill me first." I really liked that guy. He was my first love. I was so terrified of my secrets. I kept a bag packed under my bed in case I had to jump out of a window in the night if Willie found out. I also kept my bedroom door locked at all times. Once Willie took my door off for two weeks because I slammed it.

I first realized how dangerous it was to be gay at the city market in Norfolk, Virginia, in the early 1950s. I was 14 and selling produce from a parked truck in the marketplace. Many young boys from our area in

North Carolina made money this way. We slept in the cabin of our trucks at night and used the city facilities for showers and toilets, pressing our quarters into slots to pay for the services. We took our meals at the counters of local five and dime stores and our bosses came at night to replenish the trucks with produce. At the end of the week, I would return home to be with my family on Saturday and Sunday nights. Then Monday mornings I would ride with the farmer, restock the truck, and drive back to the city market, where he would leave me with the truck for the week.

Two young Marines stopped by my truck every day for tomatoes, apples, and peaches. They ate their purchases while chatting with me, friendly and handsome in their uniforms. I liked them a lot. One afternoon as I was closing down my truck for the day, they appeared and asked if I'd like to go to an amusement park called City Park with them. I was so thrilled to be asked to hang out with these nice older men in their uniforms so I didn't worry about going with them. I felt grown up, safe and excited that they wanted to include me. It never occurred to me that they might be gay. I wasn't even sure I was at that point, even though I knew I had some tendencies and experiences. I soon found out that I had no experiences at all.

We went off and had a wonderful time at the fair. Walking back to my truck, one of the guys said he needed to relieve himself and went off to a dark corner on the street. The other one stayed with me. Then the one who had gone to the corner called after me and asked me to come over to him and in the moment I was curious so I went. The next thing I knew, I woke up on my back in the middle of the street looking up at the many concerned faces staring down at me. As I lay on the ground, I began to scream and cry, asking for my Uncle Vannie, who lived not far away.

Finally, someone realized I was in need of help and called the police. The officers asked me what happened, and I told them. All the truck money was gone, along with a watch my grandmother had just given me for my birthday. I told the officer that the men had tried to have sexual contact with me before I was knocked out. I recalled feeling an electric shock go through me right before I lost consciousness. But the police didn't want to talk about the sexual encounter and told me not to say anything more about it. They said it was not important. "Do not mention that again boy!" Well, it was 1954.

The officers put me in their squad car and started looking for the Marines. They drove me around for a bit before I spotted the two guys on the street and I said to the police, "There they are, those are the ones!" The policed turned on their sirens, jumped out, and stopped the two men. They found the stolen cash and watch in the Marines' pockets and they were arrested on the spot and eventually found guilty in a court of law.

They were then tried by the military and sent to prison.

I felt sorry for them because I had liked them. They had been so nice to me and I needed that; I was a lonely boy. Sadly, after the fact, I fantasized about being in love with them and I could not believe they would hurt me. I never told anyone else about the sexual encounter after the police told me not to mention it. I certainly never told Willie or Tillie. But that experience taught me a lesson that has protected me my whole life; how not to trust so much and to think things through. I will never forget how lucky I was that night and what happened to me in that dark street in the Norfolk Virginia Farmers Market. It also was the first time I thought about writing, but I was too scared to tell the story then.

I moved around Poplar Branch very carefully from then on. I was never mistreated or abused by my friends. I was popular in school. When I was 14 years old I had already had sex with a couple of girls. They were friends and I initiated it for the most part but they were willing to go along. After my experience with the Marines in the park, I decided at age 15 that I'd better get a girlfriend. I still liked boys better, but I wanted to seem normal so I kissed and dated, but didn't have sex anymore with any girls. I had a steady girl through 11th and 12th grades, just for show. It was so wrong, but I did not know how to handle my situation and I was very afraid.

One day I came home from school very excited and told Willie that I'd made the team. "What position are you playing," he asked. "No, dad, I don't have a position, I made the cheerleading team!" He said, "Roy, what in the hell is wrong with you "BOY?" I thought it was probably time to mow the yard. Times were strange for me.

I was driving a 1931 Ford in the summer of 1956 and was almost out of gas. I stopped at Collin's gas station and asked Mr. Collins for 25 cents worth of gas. He said, "Roy, I'll give you a dollar's worth of gas if you'll do me a favor." That was a big deal: I'd never had a whole dollar's worth of gas at any one point before that. "What do you need?" I asked. He explained that his cat had been hit by a car and was in bad shape and asked if I could kill the cat for him. I thought for a minute and then asked to see the cat. Mr. Collins had dug a hole and put the cat in it. The cat was in pain and sad to look at. I took the mallet Mr. Collins gave me, closed my eyes, and killed the cat. Mr. Collins buried it because I couldn't look at it again.

I got my dollars' worth of gas and cried all the way home. I never told a living soul what I did that day for a buck. I can still see the cat's face looking up at us as if to say "please help me" but I do not think she was saying "kill me". I have forgiven myself but it took a very long time.

Anyway, I left Poplar Branch before I really got into trouble. I was always afraid that something else terrible was going to happen there. I knew being gay or whatever I was, in a small southern town would not be good for me, so I left as soon as I got a chance.

Chapter 4

Cover-up at the FBI

In 1957, when my 15 classmates and I graduated high school, the FBI

offered me a clerical job in Washington DC. They would recruit poor but

hardworking young people from rural areas, people they felt they could

trust to be honest, industrious and good soldiers. I was proud to be one

of the chosen out of our high school; opportunities like that were few and

far in between in impoverished towns like Poplar Branch. No

scholarships were even mentioned.

So off to DC I went. My grandmother lent me $160 to leave home on the

Trailways bus to DC with my suitcase full of clothes to start my new life. I

was very proud to be working with the FBI at the age of 17, making

$2100 a year [$18,000 in 2018 dollars]. Even though I was just a file clerk,

I felt like an FBI agent. I was so proud and confident.

The FBI helped all of us newcomers to find lodging in a building on East

Capitol Street on Capitol Hill. It was called, "Money's tourist home". I

shared a room with a boy from Little Rock, Arkansas who started work

the same day as me. He was frightened too but was as wonderful a

roommate as I could have hoped for. The room was so small we had to

push the double bed back and forth so the person on the other side could get out of bed or open his dresser. We ironed our clothes on a towel stretched over our suitcases. We each paid $18 a month in rent.

We boarded at a restaurant down the street for $50 a month, which got us a hot breakfast, a bagged lunch, and a hot supper six days a week. As we left for work every morning, we'd pick up our brown lunch bags lined up on a table just inside the restaurant door and make our way across the Capitol steps to the FBI building on 2nd and D street NW. I still can picture all those bags on the table in my mind.

So there I was, working for the FBI, and terrified my secrets might get out, that I would be fired on the spot. How funny that years later the sexuality of our boss J. Edgar Hoover would be questioned. Again I was terrified. Is there no place for me, I thought? Little did I know what was ahead.

One day, I heard my high school girlfriend was expecting a baby. We had broken up when I left for DC to start my new career. *I* saw, in that moment, a way into a "perfect" life. I could have a wife, a baby, and a career with the FBI. I would fit into society, be eligible for promotions and hold my head up high to a "normal" life. Really!!!

I told my parents the baby was mine, though he was not, biologically and that I wanted to marry the mother. My father was furious. He thought she had lied about the baby so that I would marry her. My mom backed me though, so off we went to the Justice of the Peace in Waterlilly, North Carolina. But for the two years she was in my life as my wife, my dad never once invited her to his home.

The man who married us kept looking at me in a strange way as if to say, "Boy, do you know what you are doing?" I found out years later this man was also a homosexual. He must have seen the same thing in me that he had in him and been frightened for me. But I knew exactly what I was doing. I was cheating, even though I loved her, but it was a selfish motive to marry her. I wanted so desperately to appear "normal"!

I got a letter from J. Edgar Hoover congratulating me on my marriage. Another letter congratulated me on the arrival of our precious baby boy. And when my wife got a job at the FBI too, we got yet another letter from Hoover congratulating her on the new position. It was a very family friendly environment in those days. I was awarded a $50 bill that was given to me, in person, by J. Edgar Hoover for the best service in a 3 month period. A car was sent to take me to his office. He never made eye contact and his handshake was limp and soaking wet. He was indeed strange. But my plan was working, I thought. However, I learned that you cannot escape yourself.

UNITED STATES DEPARTMENT OF JUSTICE

FEDERAL BUREAU OF INVESTIGATION

WASHINGTON 25, D. C.
September 17, 1957

Mr. Roy Wesley Barnard
Federal Bureau of Investigation
Washington, D. C.

Dear Mr. Barnard:

It gives me great pleasure to extend to Mrs. Barnard my best wishes and to you my congratulations upon your recent marriage.

I sincerely hope that your future together will be filled with happiness and prosperity.

Sincerely,

J. Edgar Hoover

A letter from J. Edgar Hoover, 1957

Because of the baby, we needed some extra money. I began to work nights as a cashier at the grocery store in our neighborhood on Capitol Hill after working my day job at the FBI. We found a lovely apartment on the second floor of a private home belonging to an elderly couple. They took a liking to us and would babysit so we could go to the movies once in a while. I would mow the yard for them; after all, I had been well trained for the job. I liked them very much.

All appeared to be well. I could hold my head high. I fit in with society and was great at acting the part, or so I thought. For the first time in my life I was a "normal, all-American male." Look at your cheerleader son now, Willie, I thought. Working at the FBI and married with children. I used my wife and her child knowingly as the perfect cover up. I was a perfect husband and I was a perfect father, having played the roles of surrogate husband to Tillie and surrogate father to my siblings. I had a perfect home, car, job, and church life ready for close scrutiny by society. Bring it on, I was ready.

However, inside I was a raging maniac. I was tangled in a web so beautifully woven by myself. Thoughts of murder and suicide crept into my mind during the dark of night. After two years I began to realize that I might be capable of doing serious harm to all who loved me because I hated myself so much. I was afraid of living the lie but more afraid of the truth! I finally told my wife I had to go and why. She said sweetly, "I can live with that. Just don't leave us." It broke my heart, but I knew I could not do that to her or myself. I had to face my demons. I thought being a queer, homosexual or whatever society labeled me, was probably "EVIL".

One night I left the apartment on the pretense of buying milk at the grocery store for our precious baby boy. Instead, I bought a newspaper and looked in the classified ads under rooms to share and never looked back. My wife begged to me stay and believed that we could work it out. I loved her as a friend, I assured her. But, I just had to go. I was afraid of myself and what I might do.

I responded to one of the newspaper ads, and boy did I luck out. The guy I contacted was also gay and he helped me immensely. I was an emotional wreck when I arrived at his apartment on 19th st. NW in DC and I cried for a couple of days. I was 19 years old and so much had already happened to me.

The guilt I felt was incredible and I missed my wife and baby so much, but I knew that if I didn't get away I would hurt either myself or all of us. I gave her all the money I had and helped her as much as I could. After all these years I'm still so sorry about my marriage to my precious wife and our baby boy. At the time I thought I was doing her a favor and I loved her. She was a loving, giving, brilliant woman. Alas, the entire situation was a cover up to deal with the society of life and I was terrified to live with my cover-up and the guilt.

Despite my leaving her, I remained friends with my wife until her death a few years ago. I also stayed in touch with our son. I always felt sad that he was too ashamed, disappointed, or simply afraid to discuss his sexuality with me of all people. How did I not pick up that there was a problem and that he was also gay? He was even more secretive and clever at disguising himself than I was.

When my son was 14, I decided he had to know the truth about me and I explained to him why I had left him at such an early age. His response to me was simply, "That's cool." It wasn't that he was without a father for very long because his mother remarried after I left her and they went on to have other children bringing siblings into his life.

He was a bright young man and eventually had a great job, a wonderful family with a terrific wife and three beautiful daughters. I love them and am committed to them and their love for me to this very day.

They had a nice house. Everything was perfect for him, it seemed. Just as I had created my artificial life, he also created his. But it wasn't enough. Remember, he was not my child by blood, but I was his Father.

I tried to find out as much as he would share with me. Unfortunately, at some point he turned away from both me, his stepfather and his blood father, as they had connected, saying he had too many fathers in his life.

At the age of 43, my son committed suicide. He couldn't live with the fact that he was gay. He had been living a double life – like the double life that I had walked away from. He experienced the same things I did, but paid the ultimate price. Suicide had crossed my own mind more than once in those 2 ½ years of being a husband and father, but I chose life and faced the truth. It was at the expense of hurting those I loved but in a different but safe way. I am to this day so thankful that I had the strength and courage to just walk away.

Eventually, I felt that the path I had chosen was making me stronger and closer to living with grace and joy in my heart. This was the beginning of self-discovery beyond my wildest dreams. I often, even now, cannot believe how I managed to survive, but am so grateful to be able to share this story.

I lived a bold, chilling, frightening lie from 1946, when I first realized I was gay, until 1959, when I dared to turn my whole world upside down and inside out by leaving my wife and coming out. I'm not sure how I survived all those years without seriously harming myself and many loved ones in my life – yes, including Willie. I'm sure that is why many people of my sexual persuasion never made it to maturity, even up to and including the 1990s. Even today, with all the media attention and openness to various orientations, sexuality is still a very private thing and many cannot cope with the truth. Many children with those tendencies, no matter the current exposure, will be terrified when they turn the lights off in their bedrooms at night. It is so very scary and not all survive even as I write this.

I quit the FBI in 1959 partly because my ex-wife worked there too and partly because it wasn't the most comfortable place for a gay person to work. I got a job working as a dispatcher for a trucking company at this time and loved the job. The drivers liked me and even though they knew I was gay they never gave me away to my boss. They even gave me advice on how to dispatch more easily so I could do my job better. They taught me how to order the trucks and drivers to the front in a manly way. Things went very well for me from 1959 to 1962.

I fell in love with my first boyfriend in 1962. He was older than me and taught me all about the finer things of life: how to be a host, how to set a formal table with fine china and crystal, but most importantly how to be really carefree and share with people. For a few years I was happy with my new life. I lived in Alexandria and shared a house with two guys who were lovers and who helped me find my way in the gay underworld of Washington DC.

I returned to government work in 1967, this time with the Federal Trade Commission in the division of Export Trade. I had a nice job there and it was a great place to work. I was popular at the office. My participation in the social gatherings and FTC employee outings – decorating the Christmas tree, organizing social events – won me the title of Lord FedTRaCom (the name of Commission's social club). It was a lovely time in my life.

My boss was an alcoholic and was gone all day so we took advantage of that by taking two-hour lunches and relaxing. It was fun at first but I got depressed after a while because I wasn't being productive. After a while everyone needs a sense of accomplishment. So the search was on once more. This time looking seriously at finding a professional future since my sexual life had calmed down.

I had been interested in hairstyling ever since I'd helped my mother do her "kitchen cutting" back in Poplar Branch, NC. I remembered the companionships she enjoyed on that back porch as she chatted with her clients. So I enrolled in a 2-year hairstylist program, attending school in the evenings. That allowed my creative side to flourish. I attended the

"Warflynn Beauty Academy" on G Street in downtown DC. The owner, Mr. Paul saw something in me and became a mentor to me.

I became a personality on the gay scene. The bars were hidden away, dark and secretive, as they had to be and always downstairs. But once you were inside one, it was a welcoming environment. In those days everyone knew each other in the gay bars – the Redskins Lounge, The Derby Room, The Hideaway, The Chicken Hut. It was like a gay version of the TV series bar "Cheers" – a place where everyone knows your name and no-one judged anyone like they do in gay bars today. I loved my new found notoriety.

Howard was the piano player at the Chicken Hut. Everyone called him Miss Hattie. (He actually died at the piano there.) The first thing I bought myself, once I'd saved up some money was a diamond ring. I entered the Chicken Hut on Friday nights, Miss Hattie would interrupt whatever he was playing and strike up, "The St. Louis Blues" with the Chorus, "St. Louis woman with all her diamond rings..." My friends would applaud and the games would begin.

I started working part-time in the evenings as a waiter at the Hideaway to make money while also socializing. In those days you weren't allowed to stand up in a bar with a drink so I got tipped every time someone needed their drinks moved to another table to talk to someone. I encouraged folks to move.

One day I was coming into work and saw a man arriving in a Cadillac convertible. Of course that caught my eye and we got to know each other. Don began to ask to be seated in my section and over time we became close. One day he asked me how much money I was making at the Hideaway. I told him and he told me he would pay that amount so that I could quit the bar job and concentrate on school and my day job.

Funny, I left my wife and baby because I felt guilty about using them as a cover. But gay people in the 1940s, 50s, 60s, and even later who were gay needed cover-ups to achieve success in the business world. Men had to have wives and women had to have husbands if they were to climb the executive ladder in most organizations. Of course, straight women were fighting their own wars in the corporate world.

My new lover, Don was an executive facing exactly these issues. We couldn't go to his dinner meetings together, couldn't go to the country club together, and could barely go to church together without tongues wagging. He had to ask a gay girl to attend business functions with him. And his straight married male friends would scrutinize his dating record and ask when he was going to get married.

We were talking one night to our longtime friends, a lesbian couple. One was having the same experience in her organization. We came up with the perfect solution. The two of us married the two of them: the perfect cover-up.

We lived high on the hog for quite a while with our four paychecks and the promotions kept pouring in for the two executives: him and her. We had a beautiful home on Capitol Hill with a fireplace in the kitchen and two master suites. However, it was another cover-up. Would I ever be free?

Then one Sunday the girls announced to us over breakfast they were splitting up with each other. We were devastated. The party was over. The girls disappeared and we never saw them again. My boyfriend and I struggled on for a few months but eventually we split also. He became promiscuous. While I was away visiting my parents, he picked up a man and brought him to our home. He was beaten severely and the man stole all our clothes. His and mine. Of course he couldn't call the police and tell them how the man had come to be in our house, so we lived in fear of their return. I just couldn't live in that sort of a setting, heavy with distrust and violence. So, I packed what little I had left and moved in with a good friend.

We did remain friends though. He passed away just a couple years ago at age 86. He taught me so much in those early days, and I was able to help him out a bit because he fell on hard times. I recall visiting him in his trailer home in Rehoboth Beach a few years ago. When I sat on his single spare chair, it broke underneath me. That gave me the chance to offer a new set of chairs as repayment without offending him.

It was about this time, when I left Don, that people started asking me if I was a male model. I loved fine clothes and I suppose I had a bit of flair about me. (When I was a little boy I insisted on wearing my overalls backwards. It drove my father Willie crazy. And of course there was that dress of my cousin Madge's that I adored.) "No I'm not, but thank you," I'd reply. But they kept on insisting that I should be a model.

One day a friend asked me to drop off a letter to the fashion department of Lansburg's department store. The store had opened in Washington DC in 1860 and supplied materials for President Abraham Lincoln's funeral. They also installed the city's first elevator in a commercial building. Anyway, because I was going downtown, I dressed especially nice since that's what you did when you went downtown. When I entered the office with the letter in hand, there was a lady on the phone who motioned to me to wait. She put her hand over the receiver and asked me "Are you a model?" I don't know what came over me but this time I said, "Yes!" She returned to her phone call, "I think what you're looking for just walked in my door. I'll send him right over." She asked me for my portfolio. I told her I was from North Carolina and I didn't have it with me. She gave me a card and told me to bring it to Abby Chappel, the fashion coordinator at the Washington Evening Star newspaper. I thought to myself, what have I done. However, I decided to see this through and proceeded to cancel my shopping spree and go on this unexpected detour. When I walked into the Evening Star, Abby was there with a man. They asked me to walk up and down the hallway, turn around, put my head down, and raise my chin. Then they went into a corner to talk about me. She clearly was rooting for me; he was not. She won. I came back a week later for my first ever modeling job and three weeks later I appeared in 16 color photos in the Star's fall fashion magazine. I took those 16 photos and turned them into a modeling career that spanned 20 years.

My life blossomed in the early 1960s when I left the government and went into modeling full time. I loved the modeling industry. I have always needed acceptance and recognition and was about to get more of it than I ever expected. Was I ready?

"Body Language," a selection of modeling photos from the early 1970s

Chapter 5

Spilling the Beans

I didn't mean for my parents to know that I was gay, but as it turned out I was the one to tell them. I was living in DC at the time and was writing a letter to a man I'd met at the horse races in Virginia Hunt County. I also wrote a letter to my parents at the same time and put each of the letters into the wrong envelope. It was of course meant to be, and not an accident, but I was devastated when I realized my error. I was young and foolish and had written a lot of things to this man that, believe me, I wouldn't want anyone else's eyes to see and especially not Willie's and Tillie's.

When my friend received his letter he called me immediately. "Oh Lordy, Roi, I do hope this has a good ending but I'm not sure that's the way it's going to be." Well, I held my breath and was terrified to call home for a long time.

Finally, after a couple of weeks, my mom called me. She said, "Roi, I don't know what I really want to say to you. I have always held you up on a pedestal and now I don't think I will ever be able to put you back up there." I loved my mom to the moon and back. She was my best friend. My heart was breaking here. I started crying. "Mama, I didn't ask to be put on a pedestal and I don't want to be on one. I never wanted to be on one. There is nothing you have to do or say, just love me. That's all I ask of you. I'm the one that has to live this life and I'm terrified and scared to death that I cannot do this. I don't know how to be gay. I've never been gay before, this is the first time I have ever been gay. It is all so new to me, so I can't imagine not having your love and support." She promised to try to understand and that she would talk to the preacher. Oh boy. My mother had asked that I never talk about my being gay, especially if Willie was around, and I understood that.

On a visit home years later, I overheard a response my youngest brother, Michael, made to my mother. Michael was around seven years old at the time and he put his hands on his hips and said in a girlish voice, "Well, okay, Mother." I thought to myself, "Oh God, this one is going to be gay." Sure enough, he came out to my parents 13 years later.

I got a phone call from Willie just after Michael told him the truth, and Willie said, "I am just getting over you, Roi, and now 19 years later I have to deal with this one too." "Dad," I said, "I'm trying to recall...what was it you had to do when you have a gay son? Oh! I remember now. Love him! That's all you have to do! Just love him! **JUST LOVE ME!!!**"

"You're not going to help me, are you?" he asked.

"No. But I am going to love you, Daddy, and I am going to help my brother." He hung up with a bang.

Michael, my precious brother, had a really hard time accepting that he was gay and the charismatic religious background he found himself hiding behind didn't help things. He attempted suicide three times. I was there for him as I'd promised Willie. I finally took him into my home so he could have some peace and hopefully keep safe.

One day in the mid 1970s, we were driving home together to Poplar Branch. Michael was about 20 years old. As we got out of the city limits I asked him to drive. " I don't have my driver's license with me," he said. I said to him, frustrated, "Why do you think I invited you? For your company?!" We both got each other's humor and had a good laugh with that remark. I loved him so much. He was beautiful inside and out.

A bit of time passed, and I said, "So, Mikey, I hear you can speak in tongues. Can you do that any time you want?" He responded, "Roi, do you want to hear me speak in tongues?" I pleaded, "Yes, yes!!!" Then he cleared his throat, took a sip of coke and recited quickly but with a serious face three times, "SEE ME TIE A BOW TIE." We laughed all the way to the next town. What a love he was. We were bonded for life. However, he said, "Don't ever ask me to do that again!" I did not.

Michael stayed safe living with me and went on to have a life well spent, making many contributions until cancer found its way into his body and he died at the age of 57. He was a sweet soul. His partner and I are still good friends to this day.

Chapter 6

DC Gay Scene

As a gay man out in the 1960s and 1970s in Washington DC, I probably only survived thanks to my honesty and lack of fear. Most gay men liked me but were also afraid of me since they still had their government jobs and other establishment roles to protect. I had nothing to hide any more so I didn't have to follow the same rules, or any rules for that matter.

At the time, most gay people I met wanted to camp it up and didn't seem interested in talking about serious things like life and love and happiness. I didn't care much for going to gay bars or private clubs, which felt too much like keeping a secret. I didn't want to be a secret to anyone any more. I had lived my secret life when I was a terrified teenager and still lying when I was married and trying too hard to fit into society. To appear normal had seemed so necessary in those days. But it didn't matter anymore. "Thank God Almighty, I'm free at last!" Thank you Dr. King.

Gay clubs were mostly privately owned by other gay men and women. They had created a sub-culture and gave us new rules to live and play by. I was never any good with rules. I always broke them. So every time I went to a gay establishment in those days, I would unintentionally break a rule. The rules themselves were arbitrary: no hats, no purses, and no drag. I was actually thrown out of a gay bar once for wearing a while silk scarf, though to be fair, it *was* a leather bar.

I'd just spent a great deal of money in their restaurant before I went to the bar and ordered a cocktail.

The manager came over and tapped me on the shoulder and said, "I'm afraid you'll have to leave." I said to him, "I will leave when I finish my drink." I had just ordered a cocktail from the bartender and intended to enjoy it.

"No. You don't get it. You're leaving right now!" And he grabbed me and pushed, almost dragging me through the bar as people stared, wondering what was going on. He opened the door and shoved me into a trash can outside the door and shouted, "Don't you ever come back here, you faggot!" I thought to myself, there is no place for me in this world.

The next day, the owner called me and apologized for his manager's actions. He told me that his manager didn't know who I was.

I said to him, "I accept your apology but I am not happy with your words. I don't think the issue is because of who I am. I am just another person and no one should be treated like I was. I don't want anything from you. No free food or free drink. I appreciate your call but I'll never enter your establishment again."

I always felt more welcome in straight bars, churches, restaurants, and life in general and I went to these types of establishments during the late 1960s and throughout the 1970s. I was treated so much better and I felt good about myself. The bartenders and maître d's all loved my boyfriend, Charles, and me. We received first-class treatment in first-class places because we knew how to get it. And we treated those who served us with respect in return. As I grew with my life and gifts I never felt less than anyone or anything, just complete and honest with the universe.

In the mid-1960s I was modeling for Playboy magazine at the Corcoran Gallery of Art. When the show was over, several Playboy managers asked me if I would show them around the DC nightlife. Of course, meaning the gay nightlife in DC.

They said, "We would like you to go and wear one of our outfits."

The outfit was a purple velvet suit with a matching purple velvet hat. This was the 1960s, after all! I put on the outfit and took them to the most popular bar in town, the Lost and Found. The entire crew went up to the bar and began ordering fancy drinks on their expense accounts. All of a sudden, a man appeared and tapped me on the shoulder and told me I needed to remove my hat.

I said to him, "I'm sorry but I am not going to remove my hat." I had been wearing that hat all evening and my hair would have looked like a frame underneath. At that moment the executives from Playboy, who had overheard the interaction, told the bartender to cancel all their drink orders. We all got back into the limo and went to the Prime Rib on K street Northwest.

Prime Rib was, and still is, a wonderful restaurant. When we walked in, the bartender said, "Oh my God, Roi, I love your outfit!" We had a spectacular evening there with drinks on the house. It is because of evenings like this that I always found it was much easier to live in the straight world. No lies and no sub-culture rules to further complicate life. There were simply far fewer rules to live by and because I was not afraid to be gay – after all, I had survived Willie in North Carolina – I could sure survive being gay in DC. People respond to honesty but are confused if you try to fool them. Just be honest. It is not a difficult formula to live by once you are secure enough to be yourself and not be afraid anymore!

Roi modeling for Playboy Magazine

In the 1970s I took my mother to New York City for three days, and we stayed at the Plaza Hotel. She was in her 50s at the time. I woke up one night worried because I knew my father would kill me if anything happened to her on my watch. So I called her room to check on her. She said, "Roi, you just woke me up. Of course I'm all right." The next day I took her to Bonwit's and had her hair and makeup done and then to Bergdorf's where I bought her a beautiful black and white gown. That night I took her to the Pierre Hotel for cocktails and dinner. We danced together, mother and son. I convinced my mother that Dubonnet contained no alcohol so she had two drinks.

At one point she noticed two rich looking ladies – today we'd call them cougars – observing us. Mama asked why they were looking at us. I told her they thought she was a rich New York lady out with her very young kept man. She laughed so hard. Later that night, the next morning in fact, we were having breakfast at the brasserie and she started laughing again. I asked, "Mama, what's so funny?" She told me she'd never been up that late in her life except when she was having or tending to a baby. We both roared with laughter.

I also found out that morning that she didn't like apple sauce. There is so much one doesn't know about one's parents even after a lifetime together.

Chapter 7

Charles The First

I met Charles the First, a.k.a Charles David Stinson in late 1968, while I was enjoying a lucrative modeling career and working in the beauty business part-time. We met at the Hilton Hotel. Yep! The one where our President Reagan was shot.

I was in a good place in my life. I realized how lucky I was and was wide open to new adventures. Some in the gay community were jealous of my successful modeling career and were turning their backs on me. I made the most of my new-found notoriety. I would enter a party and I would announce,"No photos. I'm on contract." Those that didn't get my humor were turned off but I didn't waste time with them. I focused on those who responded to my humor. It saved a lot of time.

I adored the fame, power and the attention I was receiving during this time in my life. But it was a delicate balance. I knew that while all the stars in heaven were pointed in my direction, I must return to the universe all that it had given me.

One day the strange, daring, powerful, loving, and beloved Charles David Stinson entered my life. I was in the Plus One club and a strange character came up to me at the bar and said, "I love your work. I saw all your prints in the Sunday paper."

I had just finished modeling for a multi-photo spread in the Washington Post fashion section with the famous Nina Hyde. Her column was called "Hyde and Chic." I lapped up all the attention and even enjoyed the negative glances from the wannabes in the balcony. Yep! Even gays can be brutal!

Charles said to me that night in the bar, "I had a dream about you- that we're going to be partners and become famous together." I looked at his character, dressed in a jumpsuit with multiple horizontal straps that made him look like a caterpillar and didn't know what to think. When he left, I said, "Who is that guy?" My friends told me he was a local character and well-known hairstylist. I was interested but not impressed!

Eventually Charles and I bought Plus One and changed the club's name to "CHARLEROI". It was so exciting to be able to buy the place where I met the person who would become so important in the next decade of my life.

I was fortunate in those days to meet Andy Warhol. His staff told me he was interested in my joining the factory. I showed up, but fortunately for me, was terrified by the scene I found there at his studio and ran the other way. I consider myself very lucky that an angel was on my shoulder and is still there today!

Charles was relentless. He called me at home and at the Hilton hotel beauty salon, where I was working part-time. I turned down all his invitations and requests to meet. I wasn't used to such aggressiveness. Finally, one Saturday at the salon, my boss, whom I loved, said, "Roi, you've been invited to a Christmas party. This lady said she'd heard about you and really wanted you at her party." I said, "That's nice, but I don't know this lady." My boss said, "Just go Roi and have a good time meeting new people. You need to get out a little bit more. You work all the time here, you're modeling too and you never play." So I did and sure enough this guy named Charles was a close friend of hers and was at the party. He'd convinced her to ask me to come. I spent the evening talking to him. He said he couldn't get me out of his head, that he still had dreams about us, and that I was locked into his heart. I started to really look at this guy. He was a precious, gentle genius with sapphire blue eyes and a brilliant red head of hair.

I agreed to have dinner at his home the next week. He lived in a charming and cozy house in the Adams Morgan neighborhood of DC. He went all out to impress me but I just wanted to listen to him. He was exuberant, sweet and kind. He told me he had just opened a salon, Charles the First, not far from his house. He said he wanted me to be his partner because I was going to become famous and he needed my energy to complete the salon. He said he was falling in love with what he knew about me and what he was about to find out about me and was convinced our relationship was going to grow into something special.

He managed to seize my attention. I agreed to go to his salon the next day, a Sunday. I arrived at Charles the First, at 2602 Connecticut Ave. NW. in the sleepy DC neighborhood of Woodley Park in 1969, full of retired government ladies living in tall, old apartment buildings. But it contained this man's dream. It had a grand staircase leading up to the main floor, and two floors above that, high ceilings, crown molding, and huge windows overlooking Connecticut Avenue.

We had a wonderful time that day. We cut each other's hair and we talked about his vision of us and how we were going to achieve all the things that he saw happening in the future. He saw himself as the dreamer and me as the detail man. He assumed that I had agreed to his plans so I just listened to him and instead of being offended I was inspired and mesmerized by his ideas. I felt as though I was being woven into a web of a beautifully designed dream that would grow so quickly and so tightly that we'd be on top of the world.

Several hours later we went to dinner at the Mexican restaurant, Lauriol Plaza – which is still thriving today. We continued to talk about his desire to go into the future together. I went home with him that night, which was the first time we had actually slept together. I was terrified and it was not a wonderful experience. Charles stated that he was so tuned in with me that all would be well in time and that we would both relax and everything would become great. I just needed to trust him and let our first time go. He said he just knew we were meant to be and Charles the First was right. And so it began!

When I gave notice to my boss, Bernard LePrince at the Hilton hotel salon, he cried like a baby. I told him he had to let me go. I said, "Your life didn't start at the Hilton. You had to leave many people behind to find yourself where you are now. Look back on your life and realize that this is *my* time to fly and take a chance on love and a brighter, more secure future." He looked at me and said, "Oh my God, Roi, you have all the answers don't you?" I assured him that I would never totally leave him and reminded him that we'd be only minutes apart on Connecticut Avenue. I remained friends with Bernard LePrince for the rest of his life and he was proud of me as I climbed up the ladder of so-called success.

Within months Charles and Roi became the "duo" in the beauty business in Washington DC in the 70s. We were the darlings of DC society. We were invited to the big parties in Potomac, MD, and into the homes of dignitaries in Kolorama. It was a social thing to have your stylist at your dinner parties and cocktail parties in the seventies. What a ride. We became the first unisex salon in Washington DC. We were quoted in the press and our movements through town in our gold Rolls-Royce – license place "C1 R2" – were recorded in the DC media often. We were welcomed by the DC straight society and consequently shunned by the gay underground simply because we were out and fearless. Most gays in DC in those days were scared to be seen with the likes of Charles and Roi. If they were working for the government, their jobs could be in jeopardy. We were so out and free that we were frightening to these guys who had to be so careful. I understood it but at the same time I could not hold back because, WE WERE FREE! At this time I started calling Charles, "Charles Ann", because everyone said, "Charles AND Roi". I officially changed my name from Roy to Roi in 1963, to suit how I felt about myself, and my career. When I told my parents, Willie and Tillie, Tillie looked at me for a moment and said slowly, "Well boy, you'll always be R-O-Y to me!"

Charles and I jumped into the road of life and there was no stopping us as we ran through it. I even got Charles a couple of modeling jobs, which he really enjoyed. He was shorter than me so at one point we were posing on the staircase at the salon and just before the photographer took the picture, Charles moved a step higher than me so that he would appear to be taller. It was the last time I got him a modeling job. One reason for our success is that we were highly competitive!

We had a sharp sense of humor together and boundless energy. Charles had the great ideas as a Leo and as a Gemini, I got the job done. We soon had four salons; three in DC and one in Fairfax, Virginia. We had an eclectic clientele. Things were moving very fast. Eventually we owned a movie theater, a nightclub, a small apartment building, and several houses, including one for us on the so-called Gold Coast in the Carter Barron neighborhood of DC. It was a beautiful 15-room, five-bathroom English Tudor with an elevator and a guest cottage. We installed a pool with Marilyn Monroe's face in mosaic tiles at the bottom of it. We travelled all over the world. We attended the Cannes Film Festival, met people like Sophia Loren and Marcelo Mastroianni. So much was coming our way.

Home of Roi and CHARLES 70 to 79

Where it All Began

I had always loved Marilyn Monroe and it had been a dream of mine for 10 years to have her face painted on the wall of our salon at the corner of Connecticut Avenue and Calvert Street, just above Rock Creek Park. My dream came true for my 40th birthday. An artist, John Bailey, was staying with us and Charles commissioned the mural as a gift to me in 1981. It took 6 weeks for John to paint the mural and it has since been restored. It's now a landmark. Many people photograph it or paint the scene. It was even on Pokemon. We also put photos of Marilyn throughout the salon to continue the theme. People have given us their paintings and photos of Marilyn to add to the walls of Salon Roi.

Charles and I were good and kind to each other. We grew into a respectful, gentle love. People spoiled us. At Christmas, the grand staircase in the salon was loaded with gifts, not just bottles of wine but cases. Those were the generous 1970s. We were called the darlings of Washington's hairstyling industry. We attracted the media wherever we went because we needed it and sought recognition. I can still do that when I want to. We were in the papers and magazines all the time. Our staff was excited to work with us and we played out our privilege to the limits. We were beginning to service famous people like Rita Hayworth, Joan Rivers, Nora Efron, Carl Bernstein, Senator Hart, John Negroponte, Melvin Laird's entire family, and the list goes on!

Charles and Roi at play

When we first started the business we told our staff that there were no rules until one was broken. One said, "How will we know?" I said, "I will tell you!" Everyone laughed. Within two weeks one of our employees brought her dog to work, so rule number one came into play: no dogs at work. One month we would work wearing roller skates, the next month we would be in drag, then we did a week or two in turbans, a week or two in hot pants and platform shoes. We all worked and played well together. It was theater in a salon. Halloween was over the top. Actually I don't really remember working or any day feeling like a workday. I remember the fun and the parties, the nightlife and the disco fever. People would double park and run into the salon just to see what shenanigans we were up to. On Saturdays we had live entertainment in the salon. One week a seven-year-old boy in a tuxedo stood at the top of the staircase playing his violin. When *Annie* was playing on Broadway we hired a red-headed girl to sing and re-sing, "The Sun Will Come out Tomorrow." Another young woman sang opera. She was my favorite and still frequents the salon. I love both her and her mother.

Another Day at Salon Roi

The Woodley Park neighborhood finally accepted us and realized we were not really hairdressers on drugs. We just acted like we were. In those days there was a salon across the street called, "Henri." Every morning as Monsieur Henri was sweeping his sidewalk and we were coming to work, I would say, "Bonjour, Monsieur Henri," and he would reply, "Bonjour, Monsieur Roi." It made me feel like I was in Paris and walking down the Champs Elysée. Alice Roosevelt was one of Henri's clients. Her limo would arrive and the driver would carry Alice into the salon with her big hat blowing in the breeze. What a sight! I wish we had the ability to take cell phone photos then. When Monsieur Henri died I wept like a baby. I loved that guy!

The Salon Roi Marilyn Monroe Mural

I was once invited to appear on the talk show, Panorama. When the camera started rolling, the narrator said, "Roi, everyone knows you have the best shop in town. Tell me, who are some of your famous clients? Give me some names." When I refused, he was furious with me and ordered the producer to go to a break. He growled at me, "Why do you think you were invited on this show?" But that mattered less to me than betraying the trust of my customers. I refused to give names and was quickly off the show. The next day a motorcade stopped in front of the salon. Melvin Laird, Secretary of Defense, got out and came up the stairs half way and said, "Roi, class act on Panorama. Thank you for not telling that my entire family comes and that you did my daughter's hair for the wedding." John Negroponte, our ambassador to Iraq said, "Next time just tell them you cannot tell because it would be a security breach!"

As I filled my scrapbooks of "Charles and Roi" through the late 1960s and the happy 1970s, we were on top of the world together. It was, of course, too good to last. In 1979 the rains came pouring down on all that we had been. All that we were and were going to be was suddenly in jeopardy. I could feel my world begin to shudder. Without knowing the reason or what in the hell was really happening, I could feel the walls tumbling down. My positive attitude was being severely challenged. For the first time I felt uncertainty and fear and didn't understand why. I just did. I talked to no one about it. It was yet another secret in my life.

Roi and Charles at the Cannes Film Festival in 1977

My beloved Charles began behaving erratically and was becoming a stranger to me. I would wake up in my wonderful home on Sunday mornings and find strangers sleeping in the gardens and swimming in the Marilyn Monroe pool. I was just sick to my stomach as Charles would invite entire bars-full of people to our home after the bars closed. None of whom he knew personally. They were strangers in my home! I was so exhausted, terrified and utterly confused as to how this was happening in our oh, so wonderful life.

At home with Marilyn

At this point I gave up my place in the master suite and moved to a secure wing of our mansion where I could lock a door from the main staircase to the third floor so no one could get into my wing of the house without breaking the door down. I was scared for my life. Again, a feeling of doom was evolving all around me.

I couldn't figure out what was wrong with Charles. He had changed so quickly, making bad moves and showing poor judgment, not just personally and sexually, but also professionally. Fortunately, I figured out how I could protect myself. However, he was 51% owner of the salon and his decisions meant the house of cards began tumbling down. He became enamored with Erhardt Seminar Training (EST) which was fine for him but he tried to insist all our employees take the seminar. Employees were quitting and we were all angry with him. Staff was saying to me, "You better tell him to back off." Even clients were saying, "Roi, make him stop with the EST crap or we are leaving". Charles would hear none of it and blamed me for it. I was barely communicating with Charles at this time. As much as I tried not to show it, the salon was beginning to feel the stress between us. You cannot hide such things from the people you work with nor from your clients. Clients would say, "Roi, what is going on? Something is different here. It just doesn't feel like the same place." And, Oh, my God! They were so right! I wanted to run and hide and just not play anymore.

I had, for the first time to try to fake it with my clients and with my staff. I am not good at that but felt I had no choice. In utter desperation, in 1979, I put the machine in motion to separate from Charles personally. I forced the sale of our house that was meant to be our happy place for the rest of our lives. Charles was so angry with me that he began to behave impossibly. He flaunted a new trophy of a young man at the salon every week or two. I was so disgusted and angry with him that one day I even imagined that I had thrown my scissors at him as he was going down the staircase. My mental impression felt so real that I was relieved when I found the scissors were still in my hand.

Working at Charles the First those days was hell on earth. Things were so bad that I forced a mutiny in the salon. I had a great lawyer and I forced a sale of the salon too, meaning I would buy Charles out or he would buy me out. Each of the staff members had to make the choice whether to stay with me or go with him. Only one person decided he would go with Charles, so I had to buy Charles out and I did. It was hard on my staff because they loved what Salon Charles the First was and were nervous about what would become Salon Roi. I felt just like them, but had no choice. Little did we know that was the least of our worries. Time was moving on and strange things were happening. More and heavier rain was about to come down on this one lovely salon as it was to also drown many salons around the country. It was war! We did not know who or what the enemy was.

Our manager Ans was the last holdout. She had been with us for years at that point. Finally she came in one day and said,"Roi, I've made a decision. I am staying with you." She had been Charles's friend long before I knew her so she was in the middle of this horrible battle. I asked her, "How did you finally come to a decision? You're the last one." She looked at me with tears in her eyes and said, "Roi, last night at the dinner table, my husband said, "I'm sick of this, let me make it easy for you. If you want to have a good time, go with Charles. If you want a paycheck, stay with Roi." She said, "I will take a paycheck and I love you and I'm going to stay with you. We're going to take this wonderful place to a new level, a new beginning."

I cannot tell you how happy I was. As we hugged each other with tears rolling down our faces, I told her, "Ans, if you had left, I don't know if I could have continued. I might have just sold the business and gone back to work at the hotel. Who knows? But with you I believe I can go on some more and that we can be creative." It was the first time I had felt joy in my heart in many months. She stayed with me for 30 years and I will love her to my last day. She has always been a class act. She was my soldier as we faced what was ahead. She was our rock!

In 1982 Charles was ensconced in his new salon in Georgetown. We managed to remain friends through all the changes. But suddenly I was getting calls from Charles's clients saying, "Roi, there is something wrong with Charles. You've got to help him." One said, "I think he's losing his mind, he cut my hair and charged me for a perm. He really believed that he had given me a permanent." After several calls from several of his clients, I called Charles and invited him to have tea with me at the Four Seasons Hotel. It was an okay meeting. We were both cautious. I asked him how he was physically and he replied that he was having stomach problems but basically was okay. I was not convinced. I was going to a movie and asked him if he'd like to come with me. I still loved him but could not forget or forgive the harm that he put me and our staff through over the past couple of years. At the movies I became aware of a horrible odor coming from Charles and I remember telling myself, "he's dying." I knew something was very wrong.

Top doctors at Georgetown Hospital invited Charles and myself to a study group of gay activity. We were so "out"! We talked of backrooms in bars, clubs etc., and the unsanitary conditions that existed in those dark rooms. We introduced them to Jim Graham with the Whitman Walker Clinic. The clinic was a little walk up clinic on 18th street where gays could get help with sexual contact disease. A very small, quiet place.

Then the rains truly came pouring down and disaster struck on all fronts.

My personal life, my professional life, my belief in God and the hereafter, everything I was, wanted to be, and hoped for one day to be was challenged and I was terrified.

I will try to describe the nightmare that was AIDS but unless you lived through it, it's nearly impossible to describe. It was the most incredible decade of fear in my life. Very quickly my life would be altered forever. I was never so afraid, so horrified, so angry and so terribly frightened for all of us. Not just my staff, my clients, my personal friends, for me, but for the world. What a horror!

Suddenly so many that we knew and loved were sick. They couldn't sleep. They were sweating all night, changing their bedding and pajamas, taking cold showers, and were dead tired the next day. Staff would arrive at work looking like they had been drunk for a week. These were young, beautiful guys that had been fantastic hairstylists, making a lot of money and on top of the world. I watched and listened and wondered what in the hell was going on. They were so frightened and wanted me to find the answers for them. I was speechless, so I just held them and cried with them. Every day was torture for all of us and our clients. Parents of staff were calling me for answers. I had no answers.

Five men in my salon were sick and we couldn't fathom what was happening. They couldn't work, they couldn't eat, they were going to the bathroom all day. One was having a hard time seeing, one was having a hard time just getting through a haircut, and another just didn't know what to do because he was losing his mind. Someone would do a haircut and then have to rest for 30 minutes. We no longer knew how to book them because we didn't know what condition they would be in when they came to work in the morning.

I obtained my instructor's license so the female assistants in our salon could study and apprentice under me and try to cover for our sick and dying men. Each day was like being on a battlefield. We were at "war!" So many lost their businesses. I was close to losing Salon Roi. Finances were rocky for the industry. A frightening experience in perseverance. I prayed a lot.

The Staff of Salon Roi, 1981

Clients were distraught and of course blamed me for everything. One asked what I was doing to my staff. I just looked at her as if to say, what do you think I can do? We don't even know what is happening. I thought to myself that after a decade of joy, prosperity and love and with true appreciation for our good luck, suddenly total fear and chaos had become my life. I was so angry and blamed Charles for upsetting our life and rhythm. I had to divorce him twice, both personally and professionally.

One employee's mother came into the salon and with a black feather whisk, tried to put a hex on me. It was absolutely out of control. I was accused by one mother of killing her son and was barred from his funeral. It was a terrifying decade that changed my outlook on what is important forever.

Of course, I was not alone. What was happening to me was happening to many of my friends who owned salons all over DC. But since we didn't know what was happening, we didn't know how to address it. The brotherhood of hairdressing as we knew it came to a standstill. We could no longer look each other in the eye. We stopped meeting on Fridays in Georgetown for happy hour. Some came to say goodbye to me. The party was over.

Amidst this uncertain time, I felt need to see my dad. I was so lost and afraid, so off I went to see Willie. I drove down South one beautiful

Sunday in 1994, finally arriving at my old homestead in North Carolina. My Daddy, "Willie", was standing in the backyard near the old dried-up well that I drew water from as a boy.

As I was stepping out of the car, he came up to the door and said, "Roy, I have been thinking a lot about you lately, boy. Here I am, nigh on 85 years old. My friends are dropping like cornstalks on a rainy day in the field. Do I like it? Hell no! But it is a natural thing. One stalk has to get out of the field so there will be room for new ones. I get it. There has to be room to sprout up! Now, here you are, 30 years to the day younger than I am, and your friends and clients and employees are dying, just like my friends. It is not natural and it must make you a mite nervous."

I stood in the hot sun and looked into the clear blue eyes of my old Dad. It seemed like forever, and then we fell into each other's arms and began to wail and cry like babies. It was the first time my father had ever shown any sign of sensitivity toward me or my lifestyle.

Hearing his words helped me realize why I was truly nervous, anxious, and depressed. It suddenly made sense. At age 55, one might lose an occasional friend or co-worker to sickness or an accident, but it was way too soon to be losing this life force of friendships I had worked so hard to preserve. I was indeed losing my old-age friendship bank to AIDS. My friends of many years were leaving me way too fast and too soon. For the first time, I realized that I didn't know who would be left for me or even whether I would be left.

My father is dead now, but that day, he gave me his greatest gift. He broke my fever and gave my untimely rage and fear a new direction and purpose.

I am now celebrating 50 years in the beauty business at the same location with some of the same staff members who stood with me and watched our beautiful boys fall down, one by one, as we looked at each other, wondering who would be next: you, him, her, or me? It took a long time to catch my breath and see clearly the work I had ahead of me.

My co-workers and I who are left with me have a very special bond with life. We know how lucky we are to have the chance to go on. We look at each other every day. We do not speak of it, but our eyes tell the same story. It's the same quiet, loneliness, the look of, "What the hell has happened to us?"

This story needs to be told. I am not the only friend, lover, employer, or employee who remembers what AIDS has done to our lives, our hearts and our professions. It is the story of many business owners, co-workers, clients, and friends all over the world – just different faces and different places. The beauty industry lost some greats. It is just now beginning to present a new group of potential greats 25 years later. My prayer is that they will be safe in their lifetime.

I love life, and hope over the years I have become more sensitive and aware of the importance of not wasting precious time! Thank you, Daddy, for helping me understand!

VINCENT T. LOMBARDI CANCER RESEARCH CENTER
GEORGETOWN UNIVERSITY SCHOOL OF MEDICINE

PHILIP S. SCHEIN, M.D.
Professor of Medicine and Pharmacology
Assistant Director for Clinical Research

Georgetown University Hospital
3800 Reservoir Road, N.W.
Washington, D.C. 20007
(202) 625-7081

September 15, 1982

Charles D. Stinson

and,

Roi Bernard
Charles the First Inc.
2602 Connecticut Avenue, NW
Washington, D.C.   20008

Dear Charles and Roi:

I am writing in followup of our several meetings held in conjunction with representatives from the Gay community of Washington, D.C., the Whitman Walker Clinic, Howard University and Georgetown University in regard to developing a program of clinical diagnosis and treatment, as well as scientific investigation of the recently identified Acquired Immuno-deficiency Syndrome. As you know, the National Cancer Institute has recently requested applications for financial support to establish such programs. The principal intent is to determine the cause of this newly identified affliction, and to develop measurements which could not only prevent but also treat the established disorder.

The Acquired Immuno-deficiency Syndrome has appeared as a new disease during the past few years, much like the outbreak of Legionnaire's disease, and the toxic shock syndrome. While there has been a great deal of under-reporting of the problem, it is currently estimated that there are 15-20 new cases being reported each week, and the virulence of the disorder has resulted in the death of 50% of those individuals who have been correctly diagnosed. The clinical manifestations range from an acquired predisposition to certain infections such as Cytomegalovirus, Pneumocystis carinii, as well as rare forms of cancer - specifically Kaposi's sarcoma and lymphoma. The lay press has tended to focus this problem as one unique to the Gay community. Indeed, some 75% of recently diagnosed patients have been homosexuals or bi-sexual men who were very active sexually. Nevertheless, this may be simply a matter of the mechanism of case-reporting, and the syndrome is well recognized in many other populations including individuals with hemophilia, Haitian immigrants without apparent homosexual experience, users of intravenous drugs such as heroin, cancer patients receiving chemotherapy and individuals who have had transplanted organs such as kidneys. There is an essential underlying theme to all these cases, one of a profound depression of the immune system which apparently places the individual at risk not only for so-called "opportunistic" infections, but cancer as

DIVISION OF GEORGETOWN UNIVERSITY MEDICAL CENTER

The Struggle For The Cure, Page 1

September 15, 1982

well.

With the established resources in the Washington area, specifically the Whitman Walker Clinic, Lombardi Cancer Research Center at Georgetown University, and the Howard University Cancer Center, we are in a position to provide a system of clinical diagnosis and treatment for patients who are recognized to be at risk, or who consider themselves to be at risk for the syndrome as well as exploring the mechanisms by which this devastating disease arises. This would require a multidisciplinary effort including teams of physicians and scientists in the fields of oncology (cancer), immunology, infectious disease, epidemiology, and importantly psychology and psychiatry. The proposal that we would anticipate submitting to the National Cancer Institute for funding would involve three basic strata of investigation:

1. Epidemiology, with a comparison of the risk factors of the Gay community in the Washington, D.C. area with that of the need of Haitians, as well as patients with Kaposi's sarcoma in Africa. The principal intent would be to identify through the use of careful historical analyses those exposures and factors which may predispose an individual to the syndrome;

2. Diagnosis and management of the syndrome in the Washington community, including the identification of the prodromal phase and intervention with the use of treatments such as interferon;

3. Basic science investigation of the causation of the syndrome, including a detailed study of the status of the immune system of individuals at risk, as well as the determination as to whether or not the genetic code (DNA) of patients who have developed the syndrome has been altered by a possible virus such as CMV. In regard to the second research area, we would envision establishing three screening clinics in the Washington area, based at the Whitman Walker Clinic, the Lombardi Cancer Research Center and at the Howard University Cancer Center. The function of these clinics would be to not only screen for cancer, but also for serious infections including hepatitis. Those individuals regarded as at risk for the syndrome would be referred to one of the two medical centers where they would be seen in a specially developed multidisciplinary clinic with representation by experts in the fields of infectious disease, immunology, cancer, psychiatry and epidemiology.

This program cannot be successful without the cooperation and support of all members of the Gay community of Washington, D.C., and more specifically the leadership of the many organizations that represent this community. We would welcome their participation in the development of the program, and any advice they might give us in regard to assuring that the program eventually can participate in the care of those who are ultimately found to be afflicted by the syndrome. In order to be successful in securing grant support from the National Cancer Institute, an important factor will be a letter of understanding from the leadership of the Gay community stating their understanding and commitment to the project, as well as some estimate of the number of individuals that they represent in the greater Washington area.

Page 2

-3-

Please let me know if you require any additional information from me or other members of our team of physicians and scientists who are involved in developing the program.

With best regards,

Sincerely yours,

Philip S. Schein, MD

jw

cc: Dr. Lawrence Hill
Dr. Leonard Chiazze
Dr. Alfred Goldson
Jim Graham - Whitman Walker Clinic

Page 3

Chapter 8

My Chair by the Window

I wanted to be a dancer just like Rudolf Nureyev. I was graceful and was told that I could be a wonderful dancer, but I lacked the necessary discipline. I also wanted to be a pianist like the Texan, Van Cliburn. I was told by my first teacher that I had great hands for the piano, that I could probably be a concert pianist because my fingers stretched over an octave but alas, once again I had no discipline.

Modeling, acting, and the beauty business have been a great home for me. Now I want to write. I find it so hard to sit myself down and surrender to the paper and pen. But there's a lot I feel I must say. I think people may take a look at their own lives through travels with me in mine. I'm not much different than anyone else. I'm all drive with no discipline. I believe that writing is a form of healing. I have so much inside me and have felt so much in my life. I have enjoyed 80 years of feeling and touching and if I don't get some of this down on paper I just may explode into thin air. As I write, I find that I am losing the weight of sadness, loneliness and fear. I become happier as I let go of them. Releasing, but never forgetting. Writing to make room inside of me for new hope, new stories.

I have wonderful clients, great friends, and enjoy multiple places to live where I enjoy many different interests and friends in each place. Yet, I still drift in space sometimes very alone. After all the grieving I have done, I realize my life was not bad or good; it is just my life. Life is living and dealing with what is before you each day of living it. Grab yours and take control, find a way for yourself. If it is not writing, look for another way for just you and you alone. Go with it, why not try? I always say, "Get off your can't and never should on yourself! Just do it!"

I feel I am a conduit to my clients. When they get into my chair, I put a cape around them and lay my hands on their shoulders. I feel their bodies and shoulders surrender. Even before I pick up my scissors I can tell my clients are ready for Roi and I am ready for them. So little of our time together actually involves hair. I sometimes must remind my clients that they have not even told me what they think about their hair. I ask, why are they here today and what do they want from me? How do they want their hair done, I ask and how has it been the past few weeks since I cut your hair? I pull it out of them so they won't think I'm taking advantage or taking them for granted. They are so trusting and I will not break that trust.

Between the snips I have to talk about the clips. There is something to be said about feeling safe and secure and yes, even familiar. I have clients that cannot wait to get to their "familiar chair by the window" into the space they know so well. They feel safe there. I can see them and feel them take a deep and audible breath; then the coffee, water, smock, and the sudden drop of the shoulders. Sometimes they even fall asleep. I cherish this body language. It makes me love them even more. The absolute trust that clients offer me is sometimes overwhelming. I totally accept the trust that they have surrendered to with me and my scissors.

I am the keeper of secrets, feelings, facial expressions and laughter. Yes, even tears. I cry like a baby when necessary. I feel the tension drop off their bodies as they are at last finished fighting traffic to get here, finding a place to park, passing other salons (with parking) and going through all the hassles just to come here and share their lives and hard earned money with me. What an honor and humbling event. How could I ever take them for granted? They understand just how grateful I am and just how much I care. They know that I need them too. In every way.

All I have to do is get here in the morning, get ready and stand behind "my chair by the window." I must be clear of mind. My spirit must be ready to give 150% to each client. If not, I feel I am cheating them. You can receive average in any number of salons. Why not make your chair one that is extraordinary and way above average? It takes nothing from me to give to you. I have always believed that people will return to places where they have felt cared for.

Maybe it is because of these feelings that I'm about to enter my 50th year of service in the same location and the same chair by the window. I have seen many of the same people over the years, their children and now even their children's children. Success is not an accident! I was lucky enough to see it coming and I fight like hell to keep it against all odds. I can also spot danger. I know when it is time to protect my clients, to let them tell me their troubles. I want to know who is having a bad day and who is out of balance and needs temporary help. I need that for myself sometimes too. I think we sometimes treat our cars better than we do ourselves! I need to be aware that I have opportunity to help myself as well as others around me. My clients know immediately when I am a little off and will very definitely try to center me, just as I do for them. It's a beautiful dance together!

Once I put a cape on a young woman whose hair I'd been cutting for 6 months or so. Out of the blue I asked, "Are you expecting a baby?" She said, " I most certainly am not. Why did you ask me that?" "I don't know," I responded. Three weeks later she called and said, "Roi, I am going to have a baby and my husband wants to know how you knew before we did?" The only thing I can think of is that I've touched so many pregnant women in my career that I must have developed a pregnant touch! Through the privilege we have of touching, I think some of us hairdressers have assimilated a touch language.

The key is to love yourself, know yourself first. There's no faking in this industry. No one is unfixable or unknowable. We have a license to touch and I happen to be that type of person.

My manager for 30 years, the beautiful and lovely Ans, knew me so well that she could tell when I was running low on energy, becoming impatient or getting upset about something. She would walk over, tap me on the shoulder and say, "Darling, could I see you for a minute?" I would excuse myself to walk in the back room where she would be waiting and she would say, "Roi, please calm down. You do not want to go there. Take a deep breath and snap out of it. You are not making yourself look your best." I loved her for this. She really saved my butt so many times.

It is true, I believe, that people with artistic natures also have a very short fuse. I feel so badly when it happens, especially when it can be avoided by having a trusting friend or somebody like Ans to help you, to guide you. Sometimes it's okay to simply walk away when you realize an interaction is not going to end well and you have tried all your workable patterns!

Aside from all that, I do know that when I touch my clients on the shoulder, I can feel them surrender and let go. I love their trust and their spirits and their ultimate confidence is so dear to me. There is nothing like accepting trust and responsibility that goes with submission. I get it, I respect it, and when I release them they are, I believe, in a better place –

as I am.

I never realized when I started in the beauty business all the benefits: the trust, the hope, the ability, month after month, to continue with people and watch their lives grow; the highs, the lows, their joys, their sadness, the times to hold each other up. It is not just a one-way relationship. We trade off constantly, in every session the person who needs an energy boost more, whether them or me, will get it. Thank God it is mostly them! After all they are paying me! I realize they wouldn't be returning if it were always about me. I get that loud and clear. The client's time in our chairs should be about them, with a light dusting of you.

When I was the owner of Salon Roi, I would listen to my employees as they connected with their clients. Sometimes I was so proud and other times I was in shock at what I was hearing. I have seen the look on clients' faces saying, "Oh my God, could you please shut the hell up and get me out of here. I have things to do and I don't care how your date was last night!" It's hard to look at others' clients when things are not going well. We have to be there for the client. They are paying for our time and should get what they need each particular visit.

The next visit, the same client situation could be entirely different. They may be having a different day, a different week, a different month. It's called life. We simply have to be a vessel for them.

Often, the visit has a little to do with their hair, other times it is all about their hair! I remember once when I got blasted by a longtime client. I was having a hard time hearing but wouldn't accept the fact that I was losing my hearing, so I was learning how to fake it (I thought). That day my long-time client Anita, after talking for quite a while, simply turned around in the chair, looked me in the face and said, "Roi, you have not heard a damn word I've said!" I was shocked to have been found out as though I'd been shot out of a cannon. I said, "You know what my friend? You are so right. I am truly, truly sorry. However, would you accept that you just might owe me one this time?" She started laughing and said, "You are right, but get your damn ears fixed NOW. I don't want to go through this again with you."

So I did. She was responsible for me finally accepting that I needed help. I was stunned when I found out how bad my hearing really was. When I got home from my hearing test with my first pair of hearing aids, I walked into my kitchen and exclaimed, "My God, what is that noise!" My partner, Mr. Joe, said, "Roi, welcome to the world of refrigerators." I couldn't believe how loud the refrigerator sound was to me and was embarrassed at how high the TV volume had been set. I apologized to him. I felt badly that I was causing discomfort to clients and in my private life because I didn't want to accept a weakness such as losing my hearing. My father Willie was the same way. Oh no, I thought! I am becoming my father!

At any rate, we should always let the client take the lead at all times. When they pick up a newspaper, cell phone or magazine, that is our clue to back out of the picture and simply be there until they choose to engage us. You never know what someone's day is like or will be like. You don't know what their breakfast or lunch was like or where they're on their way to. They could be going to a divorce lawyer, dentist, an operation. You never know what's going on in people's minds. Sometimes I can pull it out of them because they trust me and, oh God, I respect that! Be alert, stay tuned, be vigilant, take good care of your clients. They need you just as much as you need them.

If you have no needs, then you have no wants. How sad and boring to have no wants or needs or goals. Even now as my material wants are beginning to disappear because they have been fulfilled, I do believe the only road to happiness is to give with joy in your heart. That's why when people know they are dying, they want to give family, loved ones and friends something from their own lives. As we approach the unknown we must travel lightly and yet leave some trace of ourselves behind.

A client of mine named Richard, on his deathbed was in need of a final hairstyling from me. His brother sent me to his home in a limo to cut this longtime friend's hair. After the haircut and shave, his wife and I got him settled in his own, oh, so comfortable, bed. Out of the blue he said to his wife, "Hand me that box on top of the dresser," and then to me, "Roi, I have something to show you." Out of the box he took a beautiful silver ring with a Picasso-esque butterfly on the top, sculpted in black onyx. He said, "I actually thought of you when I bought this in Mexico many years ago. I want you to have it. Here, try it on." I put it upon my ring finger and it fit as though it had been made just for me.

I could hardly control my emotions. I thanked him and started walking out of the room gazing at my new treasure when Richard said, "Oh no, Roi, you don't get the ring until I am dead!" I was so embarrassed and emotional that I turned and walked back to his bed where he was stretched out with a huge grin on his face. I took the ring off and in true Roi fashion, dropped it on his bed and said, "Okay Richard, have it your way." The three of us exploded into raucous laughter. I then hurried out to the limo with tears of joy running down my face. Two weeks later "the ring" found its way back onto my finger. I love it and wear it often. When I know Richard's brother David is coming into the salon to get his hair cut, I put it on and while I'm cutting his hair, he gets to wear it. It is a loving ritual that we share in silence, but our hearts are so in sync. It is this type of relationship that makes me love my profession.

One day I was cutting a long-time client's hair while he was reading the *Wall Street Journal.* He suddenly said, "Roi, can I ask you a personal question?" I said, "Sure you can! You can ask me anything you want." He said, "Well, do you think the reason that I am grossly overweight and out of shape is because I'm heterosexual?" Without missing a beat, I said, "You hit that nail right on the head, didn't you, buddy? Of course it is." We both laughed. He went back to the Journal and I back to his hair! He still comes to me after many years later. He is still very overweight and extremely funny. We thoroughly enjoy each other. I love this guy, his wife and children to the moon! So many stories, so few pages.

We hairdressers build a bond with each and every one of our clients, if we can. I have an especially sincere and honest relationship with my clients, particularly with my heterosexual male clients. They know they can trust me. I am a gentleman and I enjoy their respect with me. We can talk together about anything. My guys trust me with everything. I just so appreciate that.

Nobody wants to be gay all the time, it's so tiring! Sometimes I just want to talk to a guy without anything else getting in the way. Somehow, I can be more open and honest with my heterosexual clients than I can be with my gay friends or clients. Of course there are some that totally get me! It has always been that way for me. Maybe it has to do with being raised in a small southern town of 300 people. I was certainly in the minority. I tried very hard not to be different and to fit in with the people around me, to be just another boy with the boys and men in my community. I felt very comfortable with them and was even protected by them.

I love it when clients tell me what I need to know about them. If I'm not giving them what they need, I want to know about it. I try to be realistic both as a hairdresser and as a consumer. I know what to expect from the places I am visiting. You can't make a silk purse out of a sow's ear. But if you're in an establishment that says they can and they don't, they need to be politely told. If you're in the right place, they'll correct the situation on the spot. If they don't, that's your signal to ask for your money back. Unfortunately, you cannot charge for the time wasted. That is why Salon Roi has survived these past five decades. People tell us what they need, what they want, what they expect and desire from us and then we try to meet those expectations and exceed them. However, while doing so, we are stretching ourselves into a better more giving person. The formula works.

I wanted to run the sort of business where people leave the salon and then stop just outside the front door, lean against the wall with maybe a touch of sunshine on their faces and say, "What the hell just happened here? I'm coming back for some more of this because I feel really good right now." Human instinct leads people to return to where they have felt nurtured. Some clients tell me coming to Salon Roi is like putting on a comfortable old pair of shoes or a cozy sweater. I beg my clients to tell me what more I can do for them. Not out of insecurity but pure honesty, so I am able to give people more of what they need. So many people are afraid of rejection, so that they do not tell you all that would make them happy.

Most of us are running on low and we rarely get that full tank feeling. That feeling when you've just had your car washed and filled the tank up with gas and you turn that next corner. I love that filled-up feeling. And I want to help you get there because I know when I'm filling your needs. My own level of contentment and fullness rises. What a great feeling to give yourself away to make room for more and to start over each time with a new person with new needs. I love it when I can absolutely let go and fall into the mind, body and spirit of the client I'm dealing with at that moment. That does not happen with each and every client and sometimes only once a day. A combination of things has to connect before it happens but when it does, it is a feeling like no other. Sometimes I am so overwhelmed with love and caring I just tear up right in front of a client.

Hairdressers have a special gift. We have a license to touch. You can tell so much about another person by touch. More than just looking in their eyes. By touching you pierce their aura and you're close to the fire inside them. Touch is a language within itself. I never got this message until I had been doing hair for about five years. Suddenly I was aware of a new dimension in my connection with my clients. Some of my older clients would say, "What have you done, you seem so different?" They couldn't tell me how but, I'm sure it was because of my own epiphany and awareness of the touch and feel of each client. I don't talk much with clients about it. I don't want to frighten them or have them be intimidated by my awareness. So it is my secret, of course until now. It is a gift and tool that I'm so proud to have nurtured into a second language, a quiet awareness. It is so clear to me that it exists. I hope that some young hairstylist can get what I am trying to relate here.

It gave me a new dimension in my creating new hair designs for clients. I have known some hairstylists who were much more creative than me but they had few people skills and some actually had to quit the business because they were not growing and not knowing the reason why!

One guy I knew had a total breakdown. He called me one day and explained his concern that I was so much busier than him. He told me that he was actually a better hairstylist than I was and that he could create styles I hadn't even dreamed about. Yes, rude, but he was right. I had actually taken some classes from him. He was an architect of hair but he was distraught and in some way, broken and incomplete. I actually felt a little sorry for him as he was not fulfilling himself.

I met him one day for coffee. I explained to him that although he was a genius in the architecture of hairstyling, he was weak in people skills. I told him that when we were in school I really didn't care for him very much, but I found things about him to like – as you can find things in any person if you look long enough, deep enough and hard enough. I wanted his natural design skills. But after a while his clients would drift away to someone who could offer a more pleasant experience with above average hair skills. This "genius" lost everything because he could not interact with people. He just used people to satisfy his need to be creativity and when the client would interfere he was totally lost and dismissed them.

I sent a friend to him once because I wanted her to experience his techniques. I had explained his personality to her. She went to his salon and waited till he finally came to her. He made no eye contact with her. He pushed her head around side to side, up-down and then he said, "I'm sorry, there's nothing I can do for you," and just walked away from the chair. She got in a cab, still wearing his salon robe and came to my shop in tears. I called him and said, "How could you do that to my friend. You told her that she was hopeless. You don't do that to human beings! You don't give them the feeling of hopelessness." He hung up on me.

Hair dressing in itself is a learned profession. You can be taught to do hair, but you cannot be taught to do people. So if you're good with hair but don't care much about people, please don't go into the hairdressing industry. You will have already lost. It truly is the wrong profession for you. Everyone's time would be wasted: yours, the clients' and the salon owner's. Inevitably and eventually the client will realize that your touch is not what they are looking for and they will seek a new stylist. My friend eventually had a complete nervous breakdown and disappeared from the hairdressing industry.

When I first got into teaching cosmetology – I told my students, " I choose to teach so that I can keep learning. You cannot teach if you cannot learn." I implored my students to teach me what they knew after I had shown them my way first. Then they could give me their ideas and visions and perhaps, a better way. We have to learn the physical styling of hair on manikins. So, I suggest if you don't like people but like hair, work in a wig store. The first time I actually cut a client's hair in the school salon, I excused myself and was very ill in the bathroom. That happened only with my first paying client, thank God! She stayed with me for 30 years, her granddaughter stops in to say hello often. We are friends on Facebook.

I did have a similar experience when I was invited to appear with football star Joe Theismann and the journalist Judy Bachrach on a TV talk show called, "Take it From Here", hosted by Jim Beck. The episode was a show about self-confidence. I was so happy to promote the salon and figured the host would focus on the famous people on the panel and I could just nod and agree with what they said. But as the show started the host turned to me and said, "Well, Roi, everyone in DC knows of your self-confidence, so what does it mean to you? What can you tell us about confidence?"

At first I froze but then I said simply, "I'm here! Confidence was showing up to do this show when 20 minutes ago I was in my car ready to throw up!" They all laughed and I realized life really is all about showing up. Just show up and do your job, appear on TV. Whatever! "Just do it!" Be yourself. If it was yourself who got you there, yourself will carry you through one more episode of your life!

In my early days in the hairdressing industry I traveled with the owner of the salon I was working in to hair shows and around the country. It was like a bizarre circus of hairstyling. The idea was to grab the attention of the hairstylists who came to these hair shows. So your demonstrations had to be outrageous. You had to keep their interest long enough to sell them your product and your ideas. Since I was learning how to build my self-confidence, I used things like turbans, props, lots of jewelry – anything I could do to interest the masses and hold their attention as I hid behind something until I found myself. I was very good at it and usually had the largest crowd at my stations. I loved that. I've always been highly competitive. To this day I still have to learn to keep up with what is new. I do not want to be the old man at his "chair by the window"!

However, after gaining all that attention and loyalty, not to mention self-confidence, I decided it was time to jump into the salon game myself. So I, with my partner opened our first salons and began a career in DC and Virginia. What a ride I was about to enter. How lucky I have been.

Ans, my manager and I, had always said if one of us went, both of us would go. Ans decided to retire in 2007, not because she wasn't happy but because her husband was retired and wanted her to be able to travel with him and enjoy life. She was irreplaceable, but I wasn't ready to retire myself. I couldn't imagine handling the hassles of a business on my own. So I sold the business to Daiva Kasteckaite, but requested to keep working three days a week to stay in touch with my clients and the business. Daiva freshened up the salon but retained its spirit and it was a source of joy to me to see it rejuvenated and continuing to thrive, heading for many more years of the healing arts service. We are in many ways a MED SPA. There is a whole lot of healing going on there every day without open wounds, but with love for peace in our hearts as we face another day in our lives.

On August 9th 2019, Salon Roi begins its 50th year in business at the same address with the same phone number. What an incredible history we have made for ourselves. Now the children of the original children we first served are bringing their own children to my chair by the window and we are securing our future once again. Children will always be the future of everything. We are full of life, love and talent in this joyous place. We do not have a complicated formula for success. It's actually quite simple. I learned a long time ago that most small businesses choose to be average, mediocre or minimal. I never wanted that for our salons. The salon's mantra has always been to give until it hurts and when you realize it's hurting, just go ahead and give some more. We are so excited about the coming years and have goals and plans in place so we will have that wonderful excitement of finding new roads to travel to be even more successful. We are so proud of having been in business for almost 50 years so far with several longtime employees still with us. In many ways, I truly believe our longevity has been because from day one we were and still are child friendly. Children just love our salon. I trust children.

Chapter 9

Terrible No-Good Very Best Day

Friday, the 13th of April, 1990, was probably one of the worst and best days of my life. Especially after a decade of the heavy rains of tears and horror that was AIDS with no answers and no hope.

It was a cold rainy day, just miserable outside. Inside Salon Roi was just the worst ever. The staff was all miserable, fighting, petty and obnoxious. It was like mutiny in the salon. I had worn a suit that day to try to raise my energy level. I told my beautiful manager Ans that I had to get out of the salon as soon as possible. She blocked my appointments for the rest of the day. I walked out, umbrella in hand against a deluge of rain under dark and dreary skies. I did not want to go home. A movie was not the answer. Oh God, help me!

Then I remembered how much I enjoyed "high tea" at the Hay-Adams hotel. It was 4pm on the dot, just when tea began at the hotel. I jumped into a cab and said, "Hay-Adams, please." When I walked in, the pianist was playing "Send in the Clowns," my favorite song at the time. Okay, I thought. Good! I think I made the right decision. I can do this!

The Asian guy serving tea said, "Hello Mr. Roi, I've not seen you in quite a while." Things were starting to look up. I almost burst out crying. He said, "There's a nice table for two by the piano." I said, "I'm alone." But he insisted, "Take the table please." And I did. High tea had begun. He could sense I was very needy that day. Speak of giving until it hurts, this guy was a pro.

Tea for one began arriving on my table for two. I was overwhelmed with need. Strawberries and cream, three-tier cucumber sandwiches etc...Bowls of olives, all on beautiful plates with cloth napkins. Things began to look up for me as my needs were being met so sensitively. The waiter's intuitive awareness was so beautiful. I began to wonder if I had enough money to cover such incredible service. I began to ponder what the hell was happening to me professionally and personally. Something was very wrong with me and with my employees. Was it me or them? I just did not have an answer. I simply knew that I was out of sorts and that the salon was simply not recovering from the horrible loss of the 80's. We were all angry, suspicious and oh so afraid of another epidemic. Everything had become a whisper.

About 30 minutes later, a gentleman, well-dressed with a commanding but not demanding presence entered the tea room. Everyone's head turned in unison to acknowledge the presence of such a gentleman, as did mine! I remember thinking that he was probably an ambassador or a cabinet member or a very well-to-do lawyer and I went back to my own troubled head and the beautiful tea display. I decided to call the salon to see if there'd been a revolt. The pay phones in those days were all downstairs near the restrooms as they always were in hotels. So off I went. I called Salon Roi and my manager said that all was well. Then she said, "Roi, will you please let it go? It is going to make you sick. Everyone is simply tired and the weather awful outside. It's just not a good day. Tomorrow will be a new day and we will be back on track." I told her where I was and she said, "Go back to your table, let it go and just see what happens."

On my way back to my table for two near the piano, I stopped in front of the table where "mystery man" was sitting and blurted out, "Could I assume, sir, that you're having tea alone?" He looked at me, smiled, and replied, "As a matter of fact, I am." I said, "I am too! Would you care to join me?" "As a matter of fact, I would," he responded, revealing the most charming dimples as a smile spread across his face. He said, "I will have the waiter move my setting as soon as possible." I proceeded to my table by the piano asking myself, "What the hell did I just do?" Within seconds my newfound friend, Joe was ensconced across from me. I had no preconceived ideas about this man – sexually, professionally, or in any other way. I just liked him and felt that we must meet and talk. Well, we sat there and talked for about two hours. The waiter was beside himself with delight and treated us like kings.

Eventually Joe asked me if I had dinner plans. I said, "You know what? I don't have any plans of any kind and especially today. Everything is just happening." So he suggested we go to the Mexican restaurant, Lauriol Plaza, for dinner – strangely enough, the place Charles and I had our first dinner together – and we talked for hours. Finally realizing the day must end, we made plans to meet for dinner later the following week back at the Hay-Adams hotel.

As I walked away from him in a daze I could feel my face was red. I felt hot. After all those hours of talking, I did find out that Joe was indeed gay. However, no one would ever know. He had the strongest straight persona of any gay man that I had ever known. He, of course, had much less of a problem discerning that I was gay.

The long conversations at the hotel and at the restaurant had been positive and upbeat without being invasive or intrusive. I could hardly believe that my worst day in a very long time became my most exciting day in a very long time. From hell in the morning to heaven and hope in the evening.

The next few days at work client said to me, "Roi, something is different with you? What is going on? Your face, your eyes...What in the world is happening? You look so different and you feel different." This further proves that love transforms us. I simply replied to my precious clients that I had met someone who I believed was going to be a turning point in my life if I was very careful. "I believe that I have found someone with whom I could grow old with, someone who I could love and have a learning experience with." But I felt that even if it went no further than the tea and dinner I'd already had with Joe, I had already won the lottery.

My clients were so happy for me. I was once again producing one great haircut and style after another. When you are love struck, it is amazing how everything gets better, sweeter. You forget the bad times, you forget how lonely you were. All you can think is, "Oh God, please make this work! I'm so tired of being alone and having no one to share my interest in life with."

It is a tough place to be at any age, but especially at 52 and beginning the second half of my life. I was not embracing loneliness very well. I really did not want to be alone, but was terribly frightened about embarking on another relationship. They can be so difficult. But if your do nothing, if you commit to nothing, want nothing, something will happen regardless. So whether you are alone or you jump on board with someone, something will happen, so you might as well play the game together. If it has some possibilities, just go for it and follow your heart!

Now I was feeling alive. I couldn't wait for another day to begin, to see the light of day. Everything was bright lights and lollipops again. I had renewed energy to go to the salon and take even better care of my clients and staff now that I was being so well taken care of in the enjoyment and appreciation department. When you are receiving, you really want to give. You must give. It is the correct formula for existing.

Joe and I talked a couple times every day, always with excitement and anticipation of our next encounter. Joe worked for the National Association of Museums. His boss, Tom was gay and said to Joe one day, "Joe, you seem different – happier – lately. What's going on?" Joe replied, "I've met someone and I think I'm falling in love." His boss said, "Come into my office now and sit down and tell me about this." So good soldier Joe did that. His boss said, "Okay, tell me about this person." Joe said, "Well, he's a businessman, he was a male model for very long time in DC, he works very hard, he has a lovely house at the beach and a great house here in town and is just a good guy. I really enjoy talking to him."

His boss said, "Joe, he sounds like someone I know; tell me more about him." "Well," Joe continued, "he has a beauty emporium on Connecticut Avenue and it's been there for a very long time. It's a great place. He showed it to me. It has four floors! He seems like a great business guy. He put a mural of Marilyn Monroe on his wall in Woodley Park. Mayor Marian Barry named a day in the city, "Roi Barnard Day" to honor his work on the AIDS situation." Tom interrupted, "Is his name Roi Barnard?" Joe said, "Yes, do you know him?" His boss responded,

"Joe!Roi is "NOTORIOUS! He's been doing my hair for years. He is a wild man! Please be careful, Joe." Joe said, "He doesn't seem NOTORIOUS to me."

Of course Tom had always viewed me as the young playboy who went around town with my partner Charles in our gold Rolls-Royce. He didn't think that people could actually change.

As your life changes, your needs change. When Charles died, I changed. Tom saw me regularly but never realized that I had grown and that I was no longer the bar-hopping night owl of yesteryear. People see what they want to see. No matter how much you grow or try to change your image, people sometimes only see you in the way that pleases them. Joe told me what Tom had said and then said I should perhaps be careful of his boss who didn't seem to have a very good reading of who I really was. When Tom came to the salon the next time he shook his head and said, "I can't believe this. You two are so absolutely opposite from each other." I asked Tom, " You do hope this works for me, right? And you want Joe to be happy, right?" He responded, "Of course, but I just don't get it. " Eventually after our first 5 years together, Tom changed his mind and finally wished us well. I often wondered what that was really all about. However, I won!!!

Two weeks after Joe and I met, I was at a luncheon at the Four Seasons hotel. The number one door prize that day was a three-day, two-night, all-inclusive stay at the Hay-Adams hotel. When the lady was describing the prize I told my table mates confidently, "That baby is mine!" They all smiled and dug into their shrimp cocktails. When the winning number was called out, I stood up with my ticket in hand. My table mates almost fell out of their chairs! They couldn't believe it. I ran downstairs to the phone booths and called Joe to tell him what had just happened. We were beside ourselves with glee and anticipation. Young love in our 50's was so incredible. We were so happy, so relaxed and grateful.

We checked into the Hay-Adams on Friday afternoon and had tea in the lounge and then dinner at the same table and with the same waiter when we met. On Saturday, we had breakfast delivered to our room overlooking Lafayette Park and the White House, then lunch, and dinner preceded by a mid-afternoon cognac in the lounge. On Sunday we had breakfast in the famous yellow room, went to church at St. John's across the street – the church of presidents – and then had Sunday brunch and checked out in the afternoon. We certainly made the most of our weekend.

Everyone was tuned into our joy. We had never had better service or created so many memories in a short three days. It was magical. Bob and Elizabeth Dole were there and on their way out they stopped at our table and Elizabeth said, "You boys must be southerners, dressed so beautifully." I said, "Yes indeed, North Carolina and Alabama." She said, "You both just shine bright. Wow!" Little did I know it was just the beginning of a long run of magic that now lives on in memories.

Before we met, Joe, I believe, was sliding into a life of compromise. He had settled into his job and was renting a one-bedroom apartment. I could tell he had very few friends at that time and was lacking in self esteem. He was a gentle soul, stuck in neutral and who was brave enough to let me jump into the driver's seat of what ended up being 2 ½ decades of joy for both of us. Doors of adventure opened for us. Life as I had already appreciated was beginning to change forever. All the gates were opened.

Mr. Joe, as I called him from day one, and I soon settled into our first condo. It was in Falls Church, Virginia. The Skyline Towers were famous because during construction of the towers one collapsed and several workmen were killed. The construction laws were revamped and Joe decided Skyline was probably the safest high-rise condo in the metropolitan area. Joe was a man who researched everything to the 10th degree. I loved that about him because I was completely the opposite. We bought a wonderful two-bedroom apartment with two and a half baths with the most spectacular views, overlooking the Capitol building and the other historical buildings lining the Washington Mall. We hosted fabulous

July 4th parties with champagne, hors d'oeuvres, and splendid views of the national fireworks extravaganza as well as many other displays in and surrounding Virginia. Every year friends looked forward to our Fourth of July parties, which became a coveted invitation.

His positive outlook somehow gave me such a sense of freedom that I really took inventory of my life. Honestly, there was nothing I wanted and didn't have. Mr. Joe always said to people, "Thank God Roi came to me with jewelry." We were so grateful to join forces together and get going with life and living once again with clear insight as to what it is important. Mr. Joe lost a partner to AIDS also. We were on the same page!

Mr.Joe brought me back to my faith in God. I was never overly religious but I am a man of faith and truly believe that there is something greater than us and that I can see my God in the faces of people who have goodness in their lives and that shines on their faces. We were a very spiritual couple. We first attended Christ Church in Alexandria, Virginia, then we went to the Church of the Epiphany in downtown Washington DC. Finally we found our spiritual home in a pew number 11 at Christ Church Christiana Hundred in Wilmington, Delaware.

We began our Sunday ritual with breakfast. Then each of us disappeared to his own dressing rooms to get dressed and would meet for coffee at the piano bar in our living room. We would critique each other's attire with smiles on our faces and honor each other for a job well done. We were proud of each other. Then we would go to church early to listen to the choir practice and to watch everyone walk in. We enjoyed seeing the familiar smiling of the congregation and bask in the goodwill everyone generated with theirs nods of recognition and acceptance.

After church we went to a special place to have brunch, usually the Mendenhall Inn in Pennsylvania, which had wonderful harpists playing every Sunday. We would sometimes stay for hours. One of Mr. Joe's greatest pleasures was to pick out a table with a family with children and instruct our waiter to offer that table dessert anonymously and put it on our bill. One Sunday, a beautiful family stopped by our table and the mother said, "You are the people who sent us dessert, I just know it. We've seen you guys come in here so many times and you always look so wonderful. We loved the treat but, why did you do it?" Mr. Joe said, "Because you give us such joy watching you with your beautiful children and how you are teaching them to be." The mother had tears in her eyes when they walked away. That is the man I was so lucky to share day and night with for 25 years!

Lunch at The Tower, 2014

There are no words to express the honor, respect, and love that I felt for Mr. Joe. Of course, there were moments of growth for both of us, but in 25 years this man never raised his voice with me, never lost his temper with me. He would occasionally go outside and walk back-and-forth for a while seemingly talking to himself as I would peek out the window. Then he would come back in the house to gently and discuss the situation. So we were able to handle each other on the spot. If I lost my cool, he retreated to his safe ground to regain his strength and composure just as I was doing inside the house. We would then mix a Manhattan with Southern Comfort and Sweet Vermouth on the rocks from the shaker in a glass on the side. Not a bad way for two vibrant homosexuals to share their time and space together.

I was hungry to be led down the path of goodness, awareness, education and be safe and free from the harm and anger so many of my friends were experiencing from the war against AIDS. Joe had lost a partner, and I had lost my Charles and many employees. By the time I met Joe in 1990, I was just a beaten wreck of a human being, who wondered as I spent time with the sick whether my own last days were rapidly approaching. I could never be sure and I was terrified. I cried, first about my struggle in my youth with Willie. Now this. Why was my journey so difficult. I had not yet accepted that it is just how life really is. Thank God I get it now and I am free. I can teach, I can share my story of fear and eventually gratefulness. Now I am sharing this with all of you.

Once I met Joe, the weight of the world was lifted off my shoulders and I knew I would be all right. I knew that I no longer could take life for granted if I was to be spared from the hell on earth that is AIDS.

Thus began my new life, one of love and forgiveness, particularly for those close to me. I had been angry with my friends for being sick. They scared me and made me feel less than and not worthy of living. How people were responding to AIDS at that time was so incredibly frightening and offensive. I thought maybe we would all be stoned to death. I was afraid to actually go out in public for a while.

But Joe told me my job was to spread goodness and mercy and to learn how to forgive. He said I was learning my lessons well and that he was so very proud of me. I hold onto those words every day of my life. The 25 years of learning new things every day from Mr. Joe Thompson are one of the true dividends of my life so far. I choose to share my joy with my friends and people I know every day. I speak to strangers. I smile at people on the street like I am giving a gift. If I do get a nice reaction, that's fine, and if I don't, I've lost nothing. It was free and I gave it away. I belong to everyone. I have no animosity against anyone. I have been set free, heart and soul. It is so easy to give when you have a sense of no debt. We are even, the score is balanced, it flows from me. Mr. Joe taught me how to find peace and to cleanse my mind, heart and soul, and continue to grow some more.

I loved learning about the history of this man and his blue-blood, "Bolling family of Greenville, Alabama," for which Washington's Bowling Air Force Base was named. A picture of his childhood home, which looks like a public library, hangs in my living room. The first time Joe took me to his home town, he showed me the beautiful houses that he would bicycle past every day. We drove down the main street, which looked like a movie set of bygone days. It is desolate now, and filled with secondhand stores and manicure salons, a skeleton of what it once had been. The old Ritz movie marquee where he would catch a matinee on Saturdays, the former elegant department stores, now all had a cloud of dust hanging over the storefronts. He told me stories of a more civil time, with little pressure, a slow life, a gentle rhythm to life in the 1940s, 50s, and 60s.

My heart was broken as this man talked about the decline of his youthful hometown. My own road in Poplar Branch, North Carolina, had never changed. It had always just been a dirt road, now paved, leading to the water that made us all happy! But I shared his excitement as he told me what the town had been like and showed me special places that he remembered from childhood. My heart was touched from his remembrance and I loved this gentle man even more.

He told me of the Sunday Easter parades in downtown Greenville, Alabama, with his aunt Myra Blackwell. I had the honor of meeting this elegant Grande dame of the south when she was in her 90s. I helped her with her soup at the Cracker Barrel as her eyes were failing her and the spoon just could not quite find her mouth. I hung onto every word she had to say. She was an encyclopedia of Southern graciousness. I was in love with her wisdom and generosity!

She let me do her hair and makeup one day before she went downtown to the bank in Greenville, Alabama. When we entered the bank, all the people stood up and acknowledged her: "Good morning, Ms Blackwell. Good morning, Myra. How are you today, ma'am? You're looking really great. Nice to see you." I was spellbound. The manager of the bank said, "Miss Myra, you look especially good today." Ms. Myra said, "Oh, it's Joe's friend Roi. He did my hair and makeup. He can do anything." The manager replied, "Well, he really did you up this morning." I have never felt so honored as a human being as I was that morning in Greenville, Alabama in the company of that generous and first-class southern lady.

Chapter 10

Travels with Joe

OR

We had the time of our lives

I soon found out that Joe had never traveled abroad and really had no desire to. His curiosity level was very low. I, on the other hand, loved to travel and before I'd met Joe had traveled many parts of the world. I've always been extremely curious about other cultures and their habits and tried to bring home at least a tiny part of each country I would visit and incorporate their ways of life into my own life here at home. After I visited France for the first time, I never wanted to eat an evening meal again before 8 or 9 pm. And I loved to have an afternoon siesta when time permitted; thank you, Spain! Of course, high tea has always been important; thank you so much England!

When I would get hyped up about traveling, Joe would become very quiet or detached. But after a couple of years I started going to travel agencies with Joe in tow and explained to him that I was going to travel and that he was welcome to come with me or I would simply go solo. He looked at me and said, "Well if I must, I guess I must, so I will." And he did!

Two months later we were heading to Europe. We flew to Frankfurt. In Salzburg we experienced the total eclipse of the sun at 12:18pm. Even the birds stopped chirping and little children sat down on the ground and were quiet. We took a train to Vienna and toured the woods with a private guide in his beautiful Mercedes while he played, "The Tales of Hoffman" for us on tape. We had dinner one night at the Bristol Hotel and were dressed in black tie because we had tickets to see the "Merry Widow" at the Grand Opera House. At the end of our meal Joe asked the maître d' if we could come back after the opera and have dessert. The maître d' said, "It would be our pleasure to have you two gentlemen come back to our restaurant. Looking like you two do, you would be welcome anywhere." When Joe asked for the check, the maître d' said "Sir, there will be no check until you return from the festivities for the rest of your evening here." We were just amazed and I must say it might have been the very first time I truly felt like a worthy grown-up. That gift of honorable trust truly delighted me.

The opera was wonderful, but the thrill of going back to the hotel for dessert was equally exciting. When we returned, the maître d' took us back to the very table where we had enjoyed a delicious dinner with fresh tablecloths and napkins awaiting us. Memories like this one happen maybe once or twice in a lifetime.

On our last night in Salzburg we had tickets for dinner and a musical interlude at the top of the city in a very old castle. We were stunned at the presentation of the quartet. We were so afraid it was going to be touristy but it was not. They played the most beautiful music for 30 minutes before dinner and 30 minutes after dinner as we enjoyed our coffee in the main room of this castle.

As the pure childlike magic of our trip continued, we next took the train to Venice, where my favorite thing to do was to ride the water taxis around the canal at night. I was able to look into some of the wonderful Palazzo's while elegant people sat around tables and toasting each other. Parties were going on every single night. I waved to people as they were sipping cocktails from their balconies overlooking the Grand Canal. I so wanted to join them. The piece de resistance was to stand in the corner of the canal that overlooked the Basilica Santa Maria del Salute. Thi is the spot where the great artist, Turner painted the canal with the cathedral in the background. I have a copy of that painting in my home. When I got back home and looked at my painting I saw it in such a completely different way. I can never looked at it again without remembering my feelings the moment I stood there looking at the Basilica. Chills ran up my spine as I witnessed this moment!

The next morning we arrived at the Venice station at 8:30 in the morning and waited for our train to pull into the station. It was none other than the Orient Express. The Orient Express would take us on a 24-hour, totally unforgettable ride to London's Victoria station. As we stood in the station watching down the tracks, my heart pounding with anticipation, the magnificent green and gold train came roaring round the curve and into the station. The porters in their green uniforms and bellboy hats stood at attention as we were practically lifted up the steps into the compartments. An octogenarian named Stanley took us to our Berth, our home for the next 24 hours. Stanley assured us that all our needs would be addressed and left us with the idea that the moon could be ours if we asked for it. I was astounded by the beauty of our Berth. The mahogany-inlaid walls, floors, sink, cabinet, and beautiful murals were all over the top. The crown moldings were like none other I had seen in my life. The perfect seating would become our beds at night. The full window made us feel as though we were outside the car and running alongside the train. For once in my life I was truly speechless. I remember my total surrender to this magnificent machine from another era, and thought, Oh my God, I am ready!

Before lunch on the Orient Express, Stanley came to our Berth and explained all that we would experience during the next 24 hours. I was in love with Stanley. He sensed the joy that Joe and I were experiencing. People who give service so well, love it when it is recognized and then they give some more. Such was our Stanley! Joe had always been a train aficionado and had been collecting trains his whole life. We had walls of model trains displayed in all our homes, and now he could add "The Orient Express" first hand.

We spent a couple of hours enjoying lunch. I would have stayed longer but Stanley assured us if we left they could begin setting up for our black-tie dinner. We returned to our wonderful cabin and watched France fly by our picture window. Mr. Joe decided it was time to take a nap but there was no way I could sleep. I was not going to miss one minute on this beautiful baby. I was busy pushing all the call buttons in our Berth, poor Stanley. He was a charmer and at $200 per hour I felt I deserved everything the Orient Express had to offer. However, I was very nice about it and I am sure Stanley understood my perspective. He seemed excited at my wonderment.

Mr. Joe and I dressed in black-tie for the cocktail hour and were proud of each other's elegant appearance. We headed off with Stanley to the cocktail car, complete with a grand piano. We were told that the windows of the car had to be removed to get this beautiful piano into the car. The pianist asked for requests and we both blurted out in unison, "Send in the Clowns, please," the song playing in the Hay-Adams tea room when we first met. The pianist turned to Joe and me immediately and truly seemed to be playing just for us. It was the best happy hour we had ever had in our lives and maybe even to this very day!

Finally we retreated back to our Berth to refresh ourselves for dinner. Suddenly it was 7:30 and Stanley was at our door to usher us into the famous dining car. It was the same car we'd been in for lunch but it looked so different, with starched white tablecloths, candles galore, and fine crystal. Lalique windows that displayed images of women walking Russian Wolfhounds were shining throughout the car. I had trouble containing myself from screaming, "Oh my God, I am in heaven!"

Our table was set for two with everything as it should be, including at least six glasses, one of which was a champagne glass. That threw me off because we hadn't ordered any champagne. After we were seated the music started with the wedding march, "Here comes the Bride." Then a bride and her groom appeared at the entrance to the dining car. Waiters came in with bottles of champagne and began pouring champagne for all the tables. Everyone stood up when they appeared at the door and toasted the couple. We found out that they had been married only an hour before right there on the Orient Express. Okay, I cried. I think I was so moved because I felt in way that this represented Joe's and my marriage, long before same-sex marriage became legal. I truly imagined what it would have felt like if we had been married on "The Orient Express"!!!

The dinner was fantastic and I cannot with all the words at my disposal describe how wonderful the entire experience was for me. Truly once in a lifetime, I believe.

After dinner we returned to the piano bar for more drinks, liquor or brandy of your choice. We chose brandy. Then off to our berth, which had been beautifully prepared for night-time with an upper and lower Berth and beautiful Pratesi Italian sheets and pillowcases. I truly was about to enter heaven.

Alas heaven did not come. I awoke at 3 am and was hyperventilating. I never knew that I had a problem with claustrophobia until that moment. Poor Joe was so upset. I was gasping for air. I panicked. I thought I would die on the Orient Express. Joe took me out into the corridor and opened the window to assure me that I could indeed breathe and reminded me that I would like to arrive in London's Victoria Station in full glory. After a few minutes I calmed myself down and we returned to the Berth where Mr. Joe gallantly took the top bunk and I settled in the lower bunk. We railroaded into Calais at the English Channel and then boarded an Orient Express catamaran to take us to Dover, where we picked up the English portion of the Orient Express. This would take us directly into Victoria Station.

On the catamaran, Mr. Joe returned from the restroom and warned me not to go. He said there were people sitting on the floor sick to their stomachs from the rough sea. Fortunately it did not bother either of us. I chose to close my eyes and sleep for that trip to Dover. Once in Dover, the magnificent English portion and version of the Orient Express was to begin.

We boarded and were taken immediately to the lunch car. When we arrived into Victoria Station, as each table finished their lunch they were escorted off the train where their luggage had been placed on the platform. We, in no way were rushed off the train and were told to take our time. The train would be there for the next six hours. All the stewards were lined up as we departed the train and to receive their generous gratuities for such an experience. Everyone was happy and we made sure our Stanley would be pleased. What joy there is in giving. That is exactly what "tips" means; "to insure proper service!" They truly did!

I will never forget how we were treated for those 24 hours. Of course it was extravagant and I will probably never do it again in my life because it was perfect and you do not mess with perfection. Sometimes you need to just become very quiet and thank God that you are able to experience something so incredibly wonderful that it becomes a whisper, soft music in your head. A secret. Mr. Joe even became quieter than usual during the trip. We made lots of eye contact; words were not necessary to express our joy. We were both aware that we were experiencing perfection.

As we stepped off the train, we saw a man in livery holding a sign that said Mr. Barnard and Mr. Thompson. It was our driver from Claridge's Hotel in Mayfair, where we were to spend the next four nights. Again, for those four nights we were truly in heaven. We were escorted anywhere we wanted to go in London in either a Rolls-Royce or a Bentley. We had a fantastic white-glove dinner at the Connaught Hotel in Mayfair. My head was spinning and I thought to myself, I want this to go on forever. And of course it has, in my remembrance of it. That is the great thing about experiences: experience it once and you own it the rest of your life. We are so in control of our living years. It just takes a little living to truly get it and know how to keep it forever.

A Nice Day at Winterthur

Chapter 11

My Life with Willie Ended Well

Every year on my birthday, I think to myself, "Happy Birthday, Willie!" Yep, my father and I were born the same day. He was the first person in my life who turned me inside out and upside down and put me on my feet again. As different as night and day I believe we were, in many ways we were the same, even twins at times. Finally, and just in time, when he was 82 and I was 52, we got to the L word, "LOVE," right. And now that I'm approaching 82, I understand him more than ever.

I was so very lucky to finish this very important chapter with my father Willie. He was a very complicated man, except in his fatherhood with his later children. I believe he was a lost man. I also believe when my oldest brother died, he just had the worst time trying to get his life back on track. A part of him was never ever completed. He was broken. I do hope that my talking with him so aggressively and my needing his approval released the negative bonds we oh, so tightly had woven around each other. In many ways I am so glad I have had this relationship. I hope it touches someone who reads this who may be having a hard time of making sense of their own situation. We often just do not have enough time to get it right. Life goes by so very quickly Especially in one lifetime we are given. I believe that because my precious mom died first, I was given the opportunity to focus on my very own Willie. I will rejoice the rest of my life knowing my father and I had enough time to make it right in this lifetime. My mom and I adored each other. We never a problem, had a type of telepathy, and always put love first. My mom's last words to me were, "You have always been my movie star." I will never forget that farewell.

Willie and I did not have a good relationship. When Willie became more vulnerable, I saw a chance to move in and make up for the time we had lost with each other. I am so very glad that we did. I would have missed a lot of loving and gentle times with this bull of a guy, who had turned into a lamb. Also I was open to receive and be patient with him as he struggled one day at the time. Our last moments together were very sweet, if not bittersweet. We made it in this lifetime. We were able to look at each other in the eyes and say, "I love you."

I believe when we say those words, we think it may render us helpless, needy, or even vulnerable. It is the opposite. It shows freedom of character, growth, inner peace and strength. These three words, "I love you" can set you free. I truly believe that a lot of the older people we see every day who are lost, mean-spirited, grouchy and uncaring are tattered remnants of not being complete, unwilling to open their own hearts to chance. They are unwilling to open their own hearts because of the "what if's..."what if you don't believe me, what if you die, if you leave? What if I am rejected, what if this person leaves me wounded? People need to deal with this themselves, with their children and their own parents before it is too late. If you have read these words, then you have a chance to take the first step in forgiveness. Go ahead, be brave, just do it!

I was with Willie a couple weeks before he died. He told me there was no reason for him to be here anymore. His job was done, his life was over, all of us children were grown and had found their own lives and everything seemed to be going okay. He was not sick, it was just time for him to let go and he did just that. He died in his sleep, no pain, no suffering. He just slipped away. All of us kids were happy for him because we knew that he was not happy living in a nursing home the last few months of his life. His work was done, he knew it and I knew it was last time I would be with him. We were saying goodbye to each other. I remember asking him if there was anything I could get for him or do for him. He looked at me and said, "You know, Roy, there is not a thing that you can do. I really appreciate you asking. I'm okay, but if you run into some of those butterscotch candies that are wrapped in that pretty gold paper, I really would like some of those." When I left him that night, two weeks before he died, I went to the drugstore and I brought him two bags of Werther's candies and took them back to his room at the nursing home. He was so thrilled. When he died, they found the two bags in his night table drawer;

he must've forgotten that he had them. Funny, I love those candies too and every time I go to the UPS store in Greenville, Delaware, I get some and always think of Willie.

He told me he was so sorry for his actions. He told me he was afraid of my strength and that he couldn't keep up with me because he only had a second-grade education. I told him, "You don't need an education to love. You were afraid to love me because I might die like Buddy and then you would be in the dark again." He agreed, and it was the most wonderful release once there was no more fight left between us two good old boys. Willie looked at me and said, "Roy, I love it when you talk. Half the time I don't know what the hell you're talking about, but I just love to listen to you talk. So talk to me, tell me some more stuff. I love when we talk." So I would just talk to him about anything and everything.

In the end, after all, Willie and I did share a lot of talking and a lot of walking together. I loved him so much and we both tried to make up for the lost time we missed in the beginning of my life. We made it up by the end of his. We were there for each other in the end. So many people miss this. A lifespan isn't long enough for some people to complete situations that life throws at them. We were lucky. We made it just in time! Please love your life folks!

Chapter 12

The Greatest Loss

In the 2008 crash, Joe lost his investments in the financial crisis. This loss upset Joe terribly, almost irrationally, since we still had enough money to live on. However, I started noticing other changes in him too.

When Joe had retired in 1995 we had bought a condo in Wilmington, Delaware, just a 1.5-hour train trip from DC, and lived there on the weekends. With the sale of the salon in the works, Joe and I bought a house in Asheville, North Carolina in 2007, with the plan that I would come up to DC once a month and work for 10 days at a time, so I could keep my regular clients.

In 2012, Mr. Joe was diagnosed with Alzheimers. So we moved back to Wilmington where life was easier and more familiar for us and we were close to most of our friends. We were welcomed back into our beloved Christ Church family.

I was terrified for him and for myself. I said to myself, "I can do this, I must be able to do this. I will be able to take care of his needs. We have the money and I have the strength and the time." I listened to the stories people told me, the horrors described in the workgroups and support meetings I attended about the massive commitment it would take to take care of this special guy as part of my daily life.

The dark clouds of Alzheimer's were beginning to rear its ugly head. I almost forgot what the past 20 glorious years had been like before this sentence of sickness befell our wonderful world. I pushed all the glamour, the special automobiles that we owned, and the trips we'd taken, far to the back of my mind. They were no longer a reality. They were just like a beautiful dream sequence. My world was becoming quieter, more challenging, more frightening. My focus was to take care of this precious, generous, brilliant soul with everything I had inside of me. After the initial shock that this was real, I was facing the end of our dream world and now staring at the fear of reality. I realized that I would need to respond to what was placed before me and I would fight like a tiger. This guy deserved all that I could do for him. I never knew a more generous, loving human being.

I did what I have always done from childhood; pulled up my britches, tightened my belt just one more loophole, and said, "Yes. I can do this and I will do this. I will not let this guy be hurt, abused or his style of daily life changed in any way." I was going to give him the very best last days that I could possibly give. Even after a good friend whose husband had the disease for eight years told me how she had experienced a living hell of physical and mental abuse from her husband who had been a lamb before Alzheimer's, I was not afraid. I had been trained for this during the AIDS war of the 80s. There is a reason for everything.

I began to see changes in my Mr. Joe. Conversations became one-word responses from my beautiful, brilliant guy. I did receive many "thank you's" from him all day; it was easy for him to say that!

One Wednesday as I was preparing as usual to return to DC to work from Thursday to Saturday as was my custom every week, everything was packed and I was headed to the door to leave the condo. Joe was always right there for a hug and a kiss on the cheek goodbye. This time I saw him standing down the long hallway just looking at me with a blank expression on his face, no movement, just standing and looking. I said, "Well Joe. I have to go now." He said, "Ok, bye for now!" I stepped closer and said, "You know, Joe, maybe we need to get someone to stay here with you during the three days I'm in DC each week." He stomped his foot and said in menacing voice, "Don't you do that to me!" That was so frightening because in 22 years I had never heard that tone of voice, the threat of harm coming from him. So I just said, "Well, not to worry, Mr. Joe, we won't do anything today, will we? It'll be okay." I shut the door and thought, "Oh my God, what am I going to do? I am in trouble here!" I was truly devastated. For a moment I was weak and frightened. I don't remember the Uber ride to the train station.

Three weeks later on a chilly December Saturday afternoon, I arrived at the train station in Wilmington my usual time, 5:55 pm. Joe had sent me a very sweet and upbeat email earlier, saying that it was a bright sunny day in Wilmington and inquiring of my state of mind and how my day had gone. I replied with a similar email and told him how I was looking forward to joining him for our traditional Saturday night Manhattans with frosted glasses from the freezer and that I would be home soon.

I tried calling Joe to let him know I was on my way from the train station but the house phone sounded strange and then I received a garbled voice message instead of his clear beautiful message. I hung up the phone. I called his cell phone and got a stranger on the phone and apologized for perhaps misdialing. The guy on the other end said he'd only had the phone for a week. So maybe I did not make a mistake or maybe my friend had just changed his phone number. Now I was getting a little anxious so I taxied home as fast as I could. There were many thoughts racing through my mind.

On my way into the condo I asked the front desk personnel if they had seen Joe today; they said "No, not today." I had previously given the front desk instructions to not let him go out without calling me but no such thing had happened to this point. As I was nearing the condo door I got a very sick, strange feeling that something was very wrong. The hair on my neck stood up like that of a frightened dog. I slowly put my key into the door. I could hear music in the background, as was Joe's usual custom. I opened the door slowly, looking down on the floor, and saw a handwritten sign that said, "STOP!" in very large letters. The sign continued: "Do not come in, go to the front desk and call the authorities. They will find me on the master bedroom balcony around the corner from the main column. I am covered with blankets. I AM DEAD." The time stood still! My heart was pounding. I believe I was audibly speaking in tongues. I cannot believe what was coming out my mouth. I was hysterical! I ran to the balcony to try to save him, thinking maybe he was about to jump. But no, he was sitting around the corner just as he'd said, so no one could see him unless they did go past the huge retaining column. He had shot himself. I screamed his name, but there was no movement under the blankets. I thought my heart would fall out of my chest. I was aware that I must not touch anything as I might become implicated in this situation in his death. So I ran to the phone to call the front desk, and I just screamed, "HELP ME!". Within seconds the apartment was filled with all kinds of officials, employees and a couple of friends who lived on the floor. I called my priest and screamed, "Ruth!" She said, "I'm on my way," and was there in eight minutes. The condo was suddenly full of strangers, as well as friends. I was inconsolable. I could only recognize my priest, Ruth.

I remembered Joe's Saturday custom of preparing Manhattans and frosted glasses before dinner so I suggested to Ruth that we partake. She said,

"Oh Lordy, yes." When I opened the freezer there was one Manhattan and one chilled glass, prepared ahead by Mr. Joe, which sent me further down the road of self-pity, sorrow, and sadness. We made it work for us and we shared the single Manhattan.

The officials were very polite and understanding. One of the inspectors said to me, "Sir, we get a lot of calls for situations like this but they are not usually in homes like this. It is beautiful here." He was trying to make me feel better. I believe he really felt sad for me. One officer tried to ask me about the gun. I said I knew nothing about the gun, which was not entirely true. Ruth asked if she could give Joe last rites. They took her to the balcony. She had already called a couple of my close friends who came and stayed with me during that whole procedure, which took hours. Eventually a man came and said to my priest, "We are ready to move Mr. Thompson to the mortuary. Please make sure Mr. Barnard is out of sight." They did. I went to the front balcony and stayed there until Mr. Joe was delivered out of the condo. I was amazed at their sensitivity.

That night I spent at my friend's house. I will love them forever for that. I was so loved that night. The officials were so soft, tender. One lady even gave me a card for grief counseling. With my Christ Church support I was so loved.

In church the next day, as Ruth was following the choir into the sanctuary before they started singing, she said in a low powerful voice, "Joe Thompson died last night. " You could hear the intake of breaths in the congregation. He was so loved there, some started to cry. The way she announced the news and the fact that we shared that horrible evening has bonded me for life with this magnificent lady. Mr. Joe was known as "the Voice of God" at Christ Church because of his incredible gift of reading. He actually had his first seizure while reading one Sunday morning so the people knew his decent had begun at the Lectern.

Three months before Mr. Joe took his life, I was going through some drawers when I noticed that the pistol and the case were not in the usual drawer, so I looked around a bit to find it. When I couldn't, I was about to ask Joe if he had seen the gun and suddenly thought, "Wait a minute, if I don't know where the gun is, maybe he doesn't either." So I decided not to mention it, worrying that if I brought up the subject of the gun it may trigger his mind and give him a clue about a way out of himself. But over the next few months after his death I found signs of the gun being moved in three different places – a dropped bullet, a forgotten wiping cloth, an abandoned case. He was desperate and was so afraid I would find out what he was planning to do.

Mr. Joe was way ahead of me and had already planned the whole thing right down to the very day. That day was the beginning of my 10 days off for the Christmas holidays. He was so careful to not let me know his plan to the very last moments.

Every single night for 20 years Joe would stretch out of his beautiful watch perfectly straight on his bedside table. I loved watching this procedure every night! The day he died, he left his watch on my matching night table on my side of the bed all stretched out. When I saw that, my heart screamed with sorrow, love, joy, forgiveness, and yes, a little fear for myself. I wondered, "Will I get through this, will I ever be able to think again? Will I look people straight in the eyes, will I tell the truth or will I lie away my true feelings?" Then I found my strength to continue with pen in hand, to release, but never forget and prayed that I could help someone else.

Mr. Joe gave me the greatest gift, the gift of his life. I was so angry with him for taking away the opportunity to use my determined commitment caring for him for rest of his life or at least through the rest of my life.

But, he set me free to fly again. How can I not use my newfound time and freedom to achieve something worthwhile in remembering him? I must tell this story so all will not be in vain. He wanted me to roll on, travel new roads, open new doors, go to unchartered waters. In sharing this, just maybe I can help someone else who is lost. I believe Mr. Joe wants me to tell this incredible story.

I'm trying very hard to be productive and to do things in his honor.

What a joy he was to me. I felt so loved and protected by his force, his

brilliance, his joy, his great sense of faith, and his terrific sense of

judgment particularly when it came to what is right and what is wrong.

He did not suffer fools. I watched and learned many times in awe! Mr. Joe

was "once in a life time!"

"Twlight"

Chapter 13

My Eyes Are on Tomorrow

Many people have asked me why I feel the need to write a book. I think of how many ways I've been touched by love in my lifetime. None of us has a perfectly smooth, normal life. It is called growth and living! We are all destined to be touched by something that will give us pause. I don't think I would have enjoyed life as much without the bumps in the road, the challenges that eventually added up to making me who I really am, what I truly think, and how I ended up responding to what happened to me every day of my life. No sleep walking for me.

I learned at an early age with losing my sweet brother at age 7,when I was 5, how precious life is and how vulnerable we all are every second. Most of us get to live pretty full lives, but it's totally a spin of the wheel, the roulette wheel of living. So I try hard not to waste too much of this precious time on earth. I have to feel productive; I have been left here several times for a reason. I believe I have been spared so far because I am not afraid to speak out. First with my voice, now with my pen.

My true joy has always been interaction with humans. I love to touch humans. I love to hold them, feel warmth, and to accept that we need each other! There is nothing else like us, not even close. We grow, we learn, laugh, we love, hate, cry, we are just complete, but complicated. So many checkpoints to consider all the time, every day memories, projections, rejections. It is all part of who we are to become as we become the good, the bad, and the ugly. We also must start over time and again, usually with new weapons of growth, loving, living and repeat until we get it right.

While writing this book I celebrated my 80th birthday. My heart is still full with gratitude to Willie and Tillie for making my visit here on earth possible. The love that has been pointed in my direction by so many all my life has kept me in the boat. But the rowing was frightening at times. I have grown beyond even my own expectations. I know the gift of healing is love, genuine eye-to-eye contact, and heart-to-heart support. I know these gifts have only been on loan to me and now it is time for me to pass these treasures on to others. So, my goal for my 80th year of life is to carefully release this wealth of love to those who might need its abundance more than I do. I am so ready to grow, love and share joy the rest of my journey. I have abundance and I must share it.

Writing this, I already feel lighter and know that deposits into my joy account are resuming. It will be my pleasure to seek out those who could use some of what has found its way to my very core. So look out, folks, Roi is on the prowl and has goodies to share with you as needed!

After Joe died, I started doing haircuts during the days of the week that I live in Delaware in addition to working at Salon Roi Thursday to Saturday, to keep my mind off how much I missed my dear Joe. People loved Mr. Joe so much that donations in his name were enough to send two students to music conservatory for one year each at our beloved Christ Church Christina Hundred.

I co-own a historic house in Milton, Delaware. I bought it before I met Joe. Since Joe died in December, the year afterwards I decided I would put the Milton house on the local Christmas house tour in his honor and to help distract me. Each of the firsts were the hardest: first Christmas, first birthday, and on and on. The joy of writing is to release but never forget, and so it is.

Epilogue

The curtains have been drawn on Mr. Joe and I must reopen them gently and look out into the world carefully to see what is next for me. I must not jump from behind the curtains too quickly because I realize I am vulnerable and not ready yet to walk on my own. However, I am getting stronger every day and I can see that there is a new day coming. I am not afraid. I have found my pen and I write to heal. I write in public. I can be alone in a room of hundreds. It scares me to write at home.

I try to do well, to be good all the days of my life on earth. I will leave behind a lot of gifts; gifts of Joe, of love, of sadness, humor. I hold the other things, the memories that completed just one life, in one lifetime, one Joe, one story.

I do so hope that all will be well with you as we keep going and sharing. So many people are afraid to make a commitment to love something, someone, anything! I can spot them on the street all the time; fearing that something may change or happen and they might be stuck holding the situation in their heart, their head and hands. Even though wedding bells say in sickness and in health, richer or poorer, it is like we don't really hear that part of our commitment to each other. All we hear is love, sex, long dinners by the fireplace, rides on the Orient Express, or a week at Claridge's like Elizabeth Taylor and Richard Burton!

As a boy I felt miscast, alone, frightened and in total discomfort except for the love of my family, my school, and my church. But without those struggles I would never have gotten where I am in my life today. I breathe with a clean heart and full of love, forgiveness, gratitude, and peace in my soul for the road I have traveled.

We surely all have a story. I am so happy to share a bit of mine with you. However, my eyes are not on yesterday. They are on tomorrow!